People Joy

by
Ian Rowland

People Joy

by Ian Rowland

First edition

Published by Ian Rowland Limited

*I dedicate this book with love to everyone
who either inspired me to write it or
helped me to get it finished*

Table of Contents

Part Two: Talking

Part Three: Refinements

Part Four: Special Skills

Introduction

"*Each person's life is lived as a series of conversations.*"

— *Deborah Tannen*

An Insignificant Book

Some people write big, ambitious books full of grand ideas.

This isn't one of those books.

It's a small book of rather limited scope and intent. In this book, all I want to do is:

- Transform and enhance your life.

- Change the world (in a good way).

That's all.

My lack of ambition has always been a source of disappointment to my friends and family.

Welcome To People Joy

What's this book about and why should you care?

To explain, here's a short story for you. Imagine that I give you a magic wand. It's a *real* wand of almost limitless power. Using this wand, you could achieve more or less anything. You think for a few seconds about how to use it. Then you wave the wand to add one grain of sand to the Sahara desert. The End.

If you *actually* did something like this, you'd regard it as a terrible waste of an opportunity, wouldn't you? You could have used the wand to achieve amazing, *wonderful* things. You had the chance to make life better for yourself and for people around you... but you threw the opportunity away.

This is exactly what happens every day — not with magic wands, of course, but with *conversations*.

The truth is that simply by knowing how to talk to people, and make the most of every conversation, you can achieve great things and make life better for yourself and for other people. Unfortunately, most people never discover how to get the most out of the conversations they have every day. As a result, most of this potential gets wasted.

In this book, I'm going to give you a new and transformative way to think about the power of conversations and how you connect with people. I call it People Joy.

Principal Benefits

Why should you care about People Joy? Because it delivers a range of important and enjoyable benefits. Here are three of the main ones (we'll look at other benefits later).

Success

Think about what you want to get out of life. Think about your hopes and dreams and what 'success' means to you personally. You might think about success in terms of wealth, love, achieving some career goals, feeling fulfilled, running your own business, having the freedom to travel and indulge your dreams… or something else.

Whatever success means to you, achieving your goals will always involve several factors, such as time, effort and luck. However, the single most important factor is always the same: **other people**.

More specifically: **other people and how well you connect and communicate with them.**

With good people skills, your path to success becomes a hundred times easier.

Without them, it becomes a hundred times harder.

People Joy is about unlocking and enjoying the magic and power of the conversations you have *every* day. It will help you to achieve the success you want.

At this point, you may want to raise an objection. "Hey Ian," you might say, "trust me, I know how to talk to people. I do it every day. In fact, I've been doing it all my life."

I hear this a lot! However, the truth is that you have probably never been shown the *real* power of conversations and what they can achieve. Conversations can raise mighty empires or bring them down. Every great achievement involves successful conversations of one type or another. Conversations are a vital part of *every* relationship, negotiation, social reform, invention and small bit of progress we've made since we all lived in caves (which in my case, since I grew up near Manchester, means since about 1965)

An Easier Life

Another main benefit of People Joy is that your life will become significantly easier and less stressful. Why? Because when you put People Joy into practice, you tend to acquire a large circle of friends and contacts — all of whom have their particular skills, knowledge and areas of expertise. This means that whenever a problem crops up, you will almost certainly know someone who has the knowledge and experience to help you deal with it. In other words, you'll have your very own personal Help Army. This applies to any type of problem: personal, social, emotional, professional or technical.

Of course, help is a two-way street, so having this large circle of friends and contacts means *you* get to help *other people* from time to time. This feels good and adds light to your life. Helping people is fulfilling and satisfying.

Professional Skills

The third main benefit of People Joy is that it helps you to develop strong professional skills. I don't know what you do for a living but I expect you'll find People Joy useful at work. It will certainly help you tremendously if your job involves knowing how to:

- Sell or negotiate.

- Lead a team.

- Be a successful manager.

Over the past twenty years or so, I've taught various aspects of People Joy to numerous clients, companies and organisations. These include Google, Coca-Cola, the British Olympics team, the Crown Estate, the Ministry of Defence and the FBI. (Fun fact: I'm the only person from outside the US ever hired to train FBI agents.)

These are three benefits of People Joy. There are others, as we'll see later on. For example, I'll show you how to talk to a complete stranger as if you're the world's greatest psychic! I'll also show you how to establish instant rapport and get along with more or less anyone — even supposedly 'difficult' people. All in all, you'll just find life more positive and fulfilling.

Definition

Definitions can be a little dull but in a book like this you're supposed to define your terms at the start. So, I'll try.

'People Joy' is an attitude.

It means being aware of the practical, transformative power of successful conversations. It also involves awareness that conversation is causation, and that people are fascinating, worth talking to and worth loving.

To practise People Joy means applying this attitude to everyone you meet and to every conversation.

Every Conversation?

In this book, when I refer to 'a conversation', I am mostly referring to four common situations:

- Striking up an enjoyable or productive conversation with a complete stranger (where this is welcome and a socially acceptable thing to do).

- When you've been introduced to someone, for example by a mutual friend, and you'd like to establish a good connection with them.

- Conversations that involve a specific purpose, such as leading a team, closing a sale, getting hired for a job, asking someone out on a date or negotiating a deal.

- Making the most of your time with loved ones, family, friends and colleagues.

I felt this was worth clarifying because obviously some conversations are rather mundane and fleeting. If it's a frantic Monday morning and someone in the street, in a desperate hurry, asks you where the bus station is, it's probably not the ideal time to try to initiate a life-long friendship. (That said, I *have* made friends with people in situations that weren't far off from this!)

Another Way Of Looking At It

Here's another way to think about People Joy. As you may have noticed, there's a lot of conflict, hate and violence in the world. Many faiths and religions suggest the solution is for us all to love one another. This excellent idea doesn't seem to be enjoying the traction it deserves. I suspect many people are in favour of the basic 'love' message but are less keen on all the presentational trappings, and theological mud-wrestling, that tends to go with it.

Maybe the answer is for us all to practise People Joy. Conversation is the opposite of hurt, hate and harm. When people are fighting, they aren't talking. When people are talking, they aren't fighting.

Conversation is causation. It can replace hate with love, compassion, fun and people actually enjoying one another's company. Perhaps it's worth a try.

Who This Book Is For

This book is for you if you're interested in any of the benefits I've mentioned so far. It's also for anyone who wants to get the most out of life, people and conversations.

If you don't spend much time talking to people, I admit you might not find People Joy all that useful. If you're a hermit, a Trappist monk, a lighthouse keeper (do they still exist?) or a stealth assassin, or a fish, by all means read something else.

Six Short Notes

Social Codes And Customs

Social codes and customs vary tremendously from one country and culture to another. Behaviour that's perfectly acceptable and welcome here in the UK, where I happen to live, might be regarded as totally inappropriate somewhere else. As you read this book, you will now and then need to adapt my ideas and suggestions to suit your country, culture and social customs. Please don't do anything that will get you into trouble!

I Am Not A Therapist Or Counsellor

In parts of this book, I discuss ways to overcome negative feelings such as self-doubt. To be clear: I am not a therapist or counsellor. Nothing in this book constitutes qualified medical, therapeutic, psychological or psychiatric advice or is substitute for such advice or guidance. This book is for people who, fortunately, do *not* need professional therapeutic help.

Nuance And Subtlety

Any ideas can be distorted and made to sound absurd (intentionally or otherwise). I know that parts of this book could, with a little twist, be made to sound ridiculous. The techniques in this book can make a positive difference to your life. However, you obviously need to apply them in a way that is sensible and nuanced. If you're getting funny looks from people, or getting arrested, you're doing it wrong.

A Note About Magic

This book occasionally refers to the world of magic and magicians. I'm not a professional magician but I'm a keen amateur and have performed magic and mindreading shows all over the world. When I give talks at conferences I often include some magical entertainment (if requested). I'm a member of the Magic Circle in London and sometimes take part in shows there.

You may or may not like magic as a form of entertainment. I know some people have a dim view of it. You may also regard magicians in general as a rather socially inept breed who spent their teenage years alone in their bedroom practising card tricks. For all I know, perhaps some magicians fit this stereotype. However, the vast majority most certainly do not. The worldwide magic community is tremendously important to me and my magician friends are among the smartest, most talented and fun-to-be-with people you could *ever* wish to meet. They all know that they have a special place in my heart.

The relevance of magic to People Joy is simply this: you cannot perform magic *well* without mastering human communication to roughly the same extent that cheetahs have mastered running. I sometimes explore and demonstrate this point in talks and seminars.

Tweak Your Expectations

Some people, when they hear about this book, expect it to contain some strange, esoteric communication techniques — especially if they know about my background in magic and mindreading. The truth is that some of the ideas in this book are quite mundane. However, they are mundane ideas *that most people don't put into practice*. This is why they're included here.

That said, some parts of this book *do* include techniques that most people don't know about (for example cold reading). So, if you're yearning for a arcane wisdom, you won't leave *entirely* disappointed.

All The Links Are On The Website

I mention many of my friends and contacts in this book. You can find further information about *everyone* I name, and their contact details, on the website: ianrowland.com/peoplejoy. I keep this information online so I can easily update it. If I mention anyone whose work you think you'd like to know more about, you know where to look.

The author performing at The Magic Circle in London

Let's Get Started!

Now that you know what People Joy is all about, we can start exploring the details. The next three chapters address the three foundations of People Joy:

- How you feel about yourself.

- How you feel about other people.

- How you feel about conversations.

I hope you'll get plenty of value from these three chapters.

DUCK

Most chapters in this book have a DUCK at the end. This stands for 'Dubiously Useful Chapter Konclusion'. I know 'conclusion' starts with a 'c'. However, I liked the idea of chapters having a duck at the end so this awkward acronym is what I came up with. Words are our servants, not our masters. If I want to torture a word, I will.

Each DUCK contains remnants that didn't fit in the main chapter or that are meant to be humorous (seldom successfully). You can safely ignore the DUCKs if you want. You won't miss anything important.

A Beautiful Typo

Earlier in this chapter, I wrote the following sentence:

'With good people skills, your path to success becomes a hundred times easier.'

When I first typed this, I got the fourth word slightly wrong:

'With good people kills, your path to success becomes a hundred times easier.'

I did consider leaving this it like that. After all, some might say it's still a perfectly accurate statement. However, since this isn't an assassin's training manual, I decided to correct it.

Rotational Tessellations

On the title page for each chapter, you'll see a little scribble based on the chapter's number (although the one for *this* chapter was based on the word 'Intro'). Here's a word of explanation.

When I was around twelve years old, I came across the amazing art of M.C. Escher and was utterly captivated by his ingenious creations. Escher's work inspired me to start playing around with 'tessellations': patterns based on repeated elements or 'tiles' that slot together in various intriguing ways. I found this a lot more interesting than doing my homework. Then again, I found *anything* more interesting than homework because my homework was a complete waste of time.

Why do I make them? I'm not entirely sure. A juggler once told me she defined juggling as 'finding the most difficult way to do the unnecessary'. I feel the same way about these scribbles and doodles. Perhaps for me they constitute a type of visual juggling. People occasionally ask me how I make these things. The answer is: slowly and in a rather clueless, 'groping my way through the dark' way that means I've no idea how each one will turn out. I'm like a chicken trying to understand compound interest.

A Bit About Me (If You're Interested)

You might be slightly curious about who I am and where People Joy comes from. It's also possible that you couldn't care less about either of these things, which is fine by me. You can skip this part.

For those who *are* interested, I've prepared two short summaries of my life and background. One is factually true while the other is more exciting but utterly fictitious. I leave you to decide which is which

Version #1

In one way or another, I've been in the communication business all my life. I don't think I chose it so much as it chose me.

During my very happy years at Sheffield university, I met Eddie Izzard (now Suzy Izzard). We wrote and performed comedy sketch shows together at the Edinburgh Fringe and elsewhere. This stimulated my interest in what makes people laugh and how to connect with an audience and make them care about what you have to say.

For my first job, I accidentally ended up in the strange world of corporate media. I spent my time working as a writer and producer. Companies told me what they wanted to say and I helped them to find the best way to say it. I helped a truly vast range of companies to sell and market everything from glue, shoes and cheese to bread, bicycles and bathrooms, painkillers, pet food and plastic pipes!

For my next career lurch, I stumbled into a job as a technical writer in the IT industry. My role was to explain big, complex things in small, simple ways. It's the type of work that any normal person would find utterly boring. However, my brain *loves* words and writing. In fact, I need to write more than I need oxygen. This being the case, I very much enjoyed my years in the IT trade as a professional explainer.

After turning freelance and other mistakes, I unwittingly became the UK Head of Sales & Marketing for an international IT company. I enjoyed the role immensely and it taught me a lot about the joys and challenges of senior management. It also taught me to strongly dislike meetings that start at 8am.

For the past 25 years, I've worked for myself as a writer, speaker and trainer. I've taught aspects of People Joy to a range of individuals, companies and organisations around the world and I've had a lot of fun doing it. I've also cranked out a few books, either for myself or as a 'ghostwriter' for others. Not to boast, but I think it's fair to say my hard work and talent have enabled me to achieve a level of global obscurity and comprehensive irrelevance that few can match.

As I have already confessed, I'm an amateur magician and proud member of The Magic Circle. In addition, I'm rather passionate about travelling. I've explored the statues of Easter Island at dawn on Christmas Day, toured the stone city of Petra and visited the fearsome dragons of Komodo Island. I've seen the Golden Temple of Kyoto, the incredible beauty of Milford Sound and the spectacular waterfalls of Iguazu. On my travels, I've met countless fascinating people and built many wonderful friendships.

Put all that in a blender, swirl it around for a while and People Joy is the result. All in all, life has taught me to be kind, to practise self-greatness, to love people and to love the transformative power of successful conversations.

Version #2

While my precise origins are shrouded in mystery, most scholars now agree that I'm probably the secret lovechild of a member of European royalty and a movie star who cannot be named for legal reasons. Exiled from my homeland for a crime I did not commit, I spent nine years, nine months and nine days studying in a remote Tibetan monastery located in the Niemalong region. It is a name that means 'Wanderer'. This was in fulfilment of the prophecy.

One morning, at sunrise, while exploring what local guides refer to as The Cave Of The Wolf, I got into a fight with a wolf. With the benefit of hindsight, and given the fairly clear name of the cave, this wasn't entirely surprising. Summoning almost superhuman strength, I somehow managed to vanquish my vulpine adversary. During this skirmish, I was forced into dark and hitherto unexplored recesses of the cave where I discovered a set of scrolls containing ancient wisdom. Returning to the monastery, I began to study these ancient texts intensively while reclining on my neat new wolf rug.

My studies paid off. In time, I learned how to levitate at will, travel through time and do some quite good card tricks. In the ninth month of my twenty-ninth year, in accordance with the prophecy, I left the monastery and embarked on a global quest to deepen my studies of human nature.

During my travels, I performed many heroic deeds but always did so anonymously, moving on afterwards while the townsfolk gazed upon my receding form and wondered where I had come from. At these times, poignant music played while a beautiful young woman from the town, sighing wistfully, thought about what might have been while clutching a small keepsake of my presence.

Though always promoting a philosophy of peace on my travels, as an 'outsider' I often found myself confronted and challenged. When things turned violent, I always won the fight in an unruffled, effortless manner using deft martial arts skills and superior, wolf-like cunning. My challengers were left gasping for breath as they nursed their injuries and rolled around in the dust.

At length, I experienced a moment of inner enlightenment. I had a vision in which The Wolf Of Revelation, together with the Fox Of Trite Symbolism and the Armadillo of Tedious Numerology presented me with nine quill pens and nine reams of fresh parchment. I knew the time had come for me to commit what I had learned to paper so that others might follow the path of People Joy. This book is the result.

None of this is true but I don't mind if you tell people that it is.

(Then again, if all of this *were* true, what better way to conceal the fact than by passing it off as a faintly humorous aside? It does make you wonder, doesn't it? Maybe that's what I *want* you to think. Are you really going to dismiss this as fiction, in a rather gullible and sheep-like fashion, just because I *say* it is?)

Part One:
The Foundations Of People Joy

1. First Foundation: About Other People

"Sometimes it's a form of love just to talk to somebody that you have nothing in common with and still be fascinated by their presence."

— David Byrne

Progress Check

Part One of this book is all about the three foundations of People Joy.

The first foundation concerns how you feel about other people.

Before going ahead, please remind yourself of the benefits of People Joy that I mentioned in the Introduction. These included achieving success (however you define it), having an easier life (by building up your personal Help Army) and developing strong professional skills. I want you to remember there's a point to all this!

The Circus Of Forever Fascination

The first foundation of People Joy is this:

People are utterly, endlessly, beautifully fascinating.

For me, people are 'the greatest show on Earth'. I never tire of meeting people, listening to them, making new connections and building on old ones.

Whenever you get the opportunity to talk to someone, I suggest that you get excited about the prospect. Being able to meet people and listen to them is a great *privilege* that can lead to many types of joy and treasure. Consider all the things you might discover simply by talking to someone and listening to what they have to say.

Think of their **experience**. They have done things you haven't done, been to places you haven't been, seen things you haven't seen and had experiences you haven't had. All this richness of lived experience is your to enjoy... for free!

Think of their **knowledge**. They know about things you don't. I'm including academic knowledge as well as practical matters such as how to put up a shelf, replace a blade fuse, organise a marketing campaign, bake a cake or help a child to read with more confidence.

Think of their **cultural awareness**. They can tell you about books, TV shows, films and music that you haven't yet come across. Who knows what gems and treasures you could discover through them?

Think of their **skills and talents**. Maybe they play jazz piano, make all their own clothes, have a private pilot's licence or play tennis to an impressively high standard.

Think of their **natural aptitudes**. Everyone's brain and brain chemistry is different, meaning we are more naturally suited to some tasks than others. There might come a time when their natural talents and aptitudes could be useful to you or vice versa.

Think of their **views and opinions**, which may or may not be similar to your own. Simply by listening to them, you might learn something you didn't know before or gain a new perspective. (I'll have more to say about the joy of disagreement in a later chapter.)

There are a couple of other things to bear in mind when you meet someone for the first time.

You have no idea what **problems** they might have faced in the past or could still be dealing with today. Maybe they've had a rough deal in life, with many disadvantages compared to you. They might have mental or emotional health issues. Maybe they've had to deal with prejudice or discrimination that you have never had to face. Not all problems or brave struggles show up on the outside.

On a happier note, think of the **triumphs and achievements** you might find in their story. Maybe they've overcome tremendous challenges or survived great hardship. Maybe they've done great things for their community. Maybe their greatest achievement is that they've raised their children really well. You never know about the invisible gold medals people are wearing round their neck.

For all these reasons and more, I believe people are utterly, endlessly, beautifully fascinating. I therefore think it's a shame how often people talk to someone they've just met with a blank expression, zero energy and flat tone of voice. We've all somehow forgotten to love and appreciate one another, to find the joy in each other's company.

When you get the chance to talk to someone, be aware of what an immense privilege this is. You've been given the chance to connect with another human being, with all of their depth, richness, talents, knowledge and experience. Let the other person (OP) sense your glow of appreciation for this opportunity. Convey your delight via your energy, your eyes, facial expression, body language and tone of voice. In other words, spread the love. This is where People Joy starts.

Here's a nice bonus: the more you appreciate how fascinating other people are, the more you'll learn to appreciate that *you* are pretty fascinating as well!

I need to add one important point. When I say people are fascinating and the greatest show on Earth, I mean *all* of them. Even the people who maybe don't look or talk like you. Even the ones who perhaps haven't enjoyed many advantages in life, never got much of an education and maybe don't look so good. It's true that some people in this life don't make a good first impression. Nonetheless, I believe they are *all* utterly, endlessly fascinating. Worth talking to. Worth listening to. Worth loving and caring about.

If you want all the benefits of People Joy in your life, and to enjoy the success you dream of, I suggest you cultivate this appreciation for other people. When you do, I promise your life will change. More opportunities will start to come your way. Your path to your personal vision of success will become clearer and easier and there will *always* be people willing to help you. Conversation is causation. Talking is walking towards where you want to be in life.

Keys To Fascination

Here are three good ways to think about how fascinating people are:

- Enjoying a mind walk.

- Maternity to diversity.

- Why dye?

They will help you to deepen your interest in the people you meet.

Enjoying A Mind Walk

Many years ago, I was fortunate enough to visit Hawaii. Unsurprisingly, I fell in love with the people, the scenery and the extraordinary natural beauty to be found all over the Hawaiian islands. One afternoon, I visited the Tropical Botanical Garden on Big Island, on the delightfully named Old Mamalahoa Highway.

As I walked around, I was aware that I was seeing amazing, extraordinary plants and flowers unlike any I had ever come across before. Some of the flowers had amazing, intricate structures that were simply astounding. For example, I saw the White Bat flower (*Tacca Integrifolia*) and the Medinilla plant *(Scortechinii)* , both from Malaysia — which happens to be a country I love. The pictures I've included on the next page don't do justice to these incredible flowers. You can find countless photos online if you want to appreciate how spectacular they really look.

This fantastic experience has become one of my favourite metaphors for meeting new people. When you meet someone for the first time, you have a wonderful opportunity to go for a walk around their mind.

Like my experience in the botanical gardens, you will find all sorts of unexpected treasure. You'll hear stories you could never have guessed or imagined. You'll hear about frowns and cheers, joys and tears, love and yearning, talents and learning, skills, thrills and battles of wills.

Even when I have conversations with people I already know, I still enjoying going for a mind walk because there are always new gems to discover. You can know someone for a long time and still learn surprising things they never mentioned before.

I regard the chance to go on a mind walk as a remarkable privilege. It's fun, fascinating and totally free! In the Dubiously Useful Chapter Konclusion (DUCK), I've included a few examples of the amazing treasure I've found just by enjoying a mind walk.

The White Bat flower (left) and Medinilla plant (right)

Maternity To Diversity

Here's another way to think about how fascinating people are.

Imagine visiting a maternity ward and seeing twenty babies lying in their cots. At this stage, there's hardly any difference between them. Now, imagine thirty years go by and, using a magical time machine, you can see what type of people these babies have turned out to be.

You'll find they have a broad range of political and religious views. Some will be hardy outdoors types while others rarely stray from their sofa, eating snacks and watching TV. Some will be artistic while others may say they have no creative talent at all. Some will dress well while others plainly couldn't care less how they look. Some will exude social confidence while others suffer from social anxiety. Some will have strong academic qualifications while others may have none. Some will be pet lovers, devoted to their frilled-neck lizard, while others don't care for pets at all.

How do we all start off so similar yet end up so different? We know that genetics, upbringing and environment play their part. However, it's still quite a mysterious process. There are many examples of children (including twins) who grew up in the *same* environment yet became remarkably *different* people. The reverse also happens: some notably similar people come from completely different backgrounds.

You are the work-in-progress result of a vast, unique set of influences, choices and turning points — and so is *everyone* else. When you meet people, take an interest not only in who they are but also how they came to be who they are. It's always an intriguing tale.

Why Dye?

Here's a third way to think about how interesting people are.

The more *different* someone is from myself, the more fascinating I tend to find them. I suppose this is largely because the more different they are, the more likely it is that they'll be able to tell me about things I don't already know. For example, one reason why I enjoy talking to women is that I know men and women have a profoundly different experience of life. I also love the fact that, broadly speaking, men and women tend to have quite a different sense of humour.

I also enjoy talking to people from a different racial, ethnic or cultural heritage because I know they'll have plenty of mind walk treasure for me to find. I was in a print shop the other day and got talking to a woman who spoke both English and Hindi. She told me how she felt about her two languages. She said English was less poetic but more blunt and direct, which was good for telling off her kids! She felt Hindi was more poetic and expressed feelings more imaginatively.

Wherever I am, I relish the chance to enjoy a good people-watching session. It can be quite beguiling to see a few hundred people pass by and realise they are all completely different — and that every difference has a story behind it. Suppose I see someone who has dyed their hair bright blue. I feel intrigued by the difference between that person's life and mine. What's the story behind that decision? I'll never know. I feel the same way when I see someone adorned with several tattoos or wearing conspicuously garish clothes.

Age is another obvious difference between people. I enjoy talking to people older than me because they have great life stories to share. However, I also like talking to younger people because they have such a different perspective on life. Plus, they can tell me about some cool new music I'll enjoy! Two of the greatest things in life are youth and experience. The essential sadness of life is that the more you have of one, the less you have of the other.

When you savour the vastness of our range as a species, and appreciate that every difference tells a story, I think you'll find the fascination follows.

Fascinating, Not Flawless

At this point, you may feel like pointing out that while people may be fascinating, they have other qualities too. For example, they can be annoying, selfish and infuriatingly unreliable. They can also be lazy, forgetful, boring, ignorant, blatantly dishonest, whiny, abusive, hurtful and unkind.

I am well aware of the fact that people can be all of these things. When I say that people are fascinating, I'm not saying they are all enchantingly perfect. 'Fascinating' is not the same as 'flawless'. Later in this book, particularly in Chapter 11, I'll have more to say about people's faults and failings and how to respond to them.

Two Problems

There are two things (at least) that tend to get in the way of finding people fascinating. The first is the natural tendency most of us have to judge people based on their looks. The second is that most human beings have a tragic addiction to tribalism.

Let's have a look at these two problems.

Looks Don't Count For Much

Some people are strikingly handsome or beautiful. It's easy to find these people fascinating and to feel inclined to talk to them. We're all programmed by evolution to gravitate towards good looks, given half a chance. (This is one area where it's fair to say the average man is perhaps more easily mesmerised than the average woman.)

It's also easy to admire people who clearly take a great deal of care over their appearance. We can all admire people who manage to look chic and stylish. Looking good takes know-how and effort and, as with any other skill in life, some people are better at it than others. However, you've probably noticed that not everyone in the world is strikingly beautiful. We didn't all fall out of the gorgeous box. Also, not everyone either knows how to dress well or makes much of an effort to do so. People can look flabby, scruffy and dishevelled — but that's enough about me.

If you want to practice People Joy, you have to learn not to pay much attention to looks. While it's nice to meet beautiful people, looks really don't tell you much and appearances can be misleading. You have to remember that *everyone* is fascinating and worth talking to. Many engaging stories come wrapped in a plain cover.

Incidentally, the importance of not being swayed by looks is a lesson that everyone in the recruitment industry learns sooner or later. Research has shown that good-looking people often enjoy an unfair advantage during, for example, job interviews. This has obvious and regrettable consequences. Capable candidates get rejected while the company hires Handsome Harry — who turns out to be as much use as a U-shaped telescope. He gets fired after two inglorious months and then the company has to find a replacement. Everyone in business knows this happens with depressing frequency.

Tribalism Hurts Us All

One of the most difficult parts of People Joy is this: you have to let go of tribalism. Unfortunately, most people find this hard to do.

Human beings are wonderful. We can perform heart transplants, take photos of Neptune and print photos on the top of cakes (surely the zenith of human achievement). Unfortunately, we also tend to see ourselves as belonging to 'us' and 'them' tribes. When I say 'tribe', I'm referring to any group that people form in order to focus on, and squabble over, our differences instead of recognising our shared and glorious humanity. These include groups based on politics, beliefs, ethnicity, 'north v south' or anything similar. We see *our* tribe as the mostly good and righteous one and blame the *other* tribe for most of society's problems — even though, curiously enough, they feel exactly the same way in reverse. This tribal mentality gives rise to division, resentment, hate and harm.

The misguided 'us' and 'them' view of the world is a remarkably persistent glitch of the human mind. If you want to practise People Joy, and reap all the benefits, you have to free yourself from the sticky, toxic and suffocating grip of tribalism. Is this *easy* to do? Not at all. Is it worth doing? Absolutely.

There are two ways forward for humanity. One way is for us all to carry on embracing the strange, hypnotic delusion of tribal thinking. The other way is for us all to mature past this delusion and recognise that we are all much more alike than we are different. I'll have more to say about this in Chapter 11.

Zero Exploitation

I've said that People Joy will help you to cultivate a wide circle of friends and contacts — some of whom might occasionally be useful to know. However, this isn't the same as wanting to *exploit* people. People Joy is as much about what you can do for others as what they can do for you. I felt this was worth clarifying.

I have zero interest in exploiting people. I'm interested in the incredible power of kindness, cooperation and collaboration — all of which start with successful conversations.

Chapter Summary

The first foundational step of People Joy is to realise that people are utterly, endlessly, beautifully fascinating. When you meet someone for the first time, enjoy the remarkable privilege of being able to talk to another human being. Don't meet them with dead eyes and a blank look. Let them see and sense that you're delighted by this privilege and fascinated by their story.

The main headings in this chapter were:

- The circus of forever fascination.

- Three paths to fascination. (Mind walk / Maternity to diversity / Why dye?)

- Fascinating doesn't mean flawless.

- Two Problems. (Looks don't count for much / Tribalism hurts us all.)

The next chapter addresses how you feel about yourself.

DUCK

I explained this at the end of the previous chapter but I'll go over it again in case you missed it. Most chapters in this book have a DUCK at the end, which stands for 'Dubiously Useful Chapter Konclusion'. It's where I put extra bits and pieces that didn't fit into the main chapter. I know 'conclusion' starts with 'c' but I wanted to use the DUCK acronym so here we are.

Mind Walk Examples

In this chapter, I said I've had fascinating conversations with people all over the world. Here are a few examples of the treasure I've found by going on a mind walk. I could mention hundreds of others.

I once took a taxi in Las Vegas. The driver, as it turned out, was of Greek descent. He told me a little bit about his family background. Before the second world war, his family had run a thriving business in

Greece buying and selling gold and other precious metals. When the war came along, his family decided to flee to America. They had to find ways to get themselves *and* all their gold and possessions to America without being caught or intercepted. It was a moving and astonishing story to listen to.

In Italy, I got talking to a man who has one of the strangest hobbies in the world. It's not the type of thing anyone could guess. He makes replicas (or forgeries if you prefer) of the famous Holy Shroud of Turin! His work is hugely impressive and thought-provoking. I once had the good fortune to visit his laboratory / art studio, with a different 'Holy Shroud', either complete or 'work in progress', displayed on every wall. It was an amazing and extraordinary experience.

An Australian friend of mine, having worked in education for most of her life, is now happily enjoying her retirement years. After many years suffering from arachnophobia, she decided to learn everything she could about spiders and study them intensively. She became an expert and was even commissioned to write a book about spiders — which is excellent, by the way! This led to a remarkably successful career as a writer. (If you're interested, the book is 'Spiders' by Lynne Kelly. All her other books are worth reading as well).

In Kuta, Indonesia, I got chatting to a bar owner who had built up a fortune from next to nothing, lost it all when the tourist industry collapsed and then built it up again. It was an amazing story, full of dramatic twists and turns, that he told me with a cheerful tone and not a trace of self-pity.

I once took a ride on the superb Aerial Tramway in Palm Springs, California, which takes visitors high into the mountains of Mt. San Jacinto State Park. After my trip, at a nearby coffee shop, I got talking to a man who turned out to be a construction worker. By coincidence, his father had worked on the original Tramway when it opened for business in 1963. He had a few interesting tales to tell about his father's experiences. He also recommended that, while I was in the area, I should make a brief detour to visit the incredible Cabazon Dinosaurs, which I did!

While visiting St. Peterburg, I had a fascinating conversation with a woman who managed a souvenir shop. Her great passion in life was ballet. Throughout her teenage years, she had worked with tireless devotion to become a professional ballerina. During one of her first professional engagements, a clumsy stagehand caused an accident that caused her to suffer a fairly major knee injury. Although she was eventually able to make a full recovery, the accident was enough to end her ballet career. Nonetheless, ballet remained her great passion and when she wasn't in the shop she said she would most often be found watching ballet somewhere or helping backstage.

A group of psychologists in Dublin once hired me to give a talk. This was good news because I love Ireland and relish any opportunity to pay a visit to this amazing country (and *maybe* sample a Guinness). The organiser of the group kindly collected me from the airport. I thought we'd probably spend most of our time in the car talking about psychology. As it turned out, we barely mentioned the subject. The organiser, I soon learned, was the world's greatest Leonard Cohen fan. During the ride, I was entertained by a rich tapestry of tales about Leonard Cohen's life and work. These stories included an occasion when my psychologist friend *almost* went to his house to meet him.

I hope I've made my point. I want you to appreciate how fascinating people are — which includes *you* — and encourage you to start going

Mr. Rex (20 metres tall), one of the amazing Cabazon Dinosaurs

on mind walks. They are amazing and free, no tickets or passes required. You'll hear stories you could never have guessed, discover all sorts of hidden depths and see there's no limit to the richness, variety and enchantment of human experience.

My Remarkable Friend John Kippen

One section of this chapter was about the fact that looks don't count for much. Regarding this point, I must mention my truly remarkable friend John Kippen. John once had an operation to remove a brain tumour. Although the operation was a success, it unfortunately left him with a partially paralysed face as well as deafness in one ear. For about ten years, John was so appalled by his own appearance that he avoided mirrors or having his photo taken. Fortunately, he was eventually able to make peace with his looks and realise that his story could help other people.

I urge you to watch John's TED talk, 'Being Different Is My Super Power: Magic Saved My Life', which runs for 12 minutes. You'll find it moving and inspirational. Watch it, enjoy it and then come back and tell me looks matter. You should also visit John's website and buy his inspirational book, 'Playing The Hand You Are Dealt'.

In his book, John mentions this quotation from Henry David Thoreau: "It's not what you look at that matters. It's what you see." I'm reminded of an excellent track by Faithless called 'Reverence' where they sing, "You don't need eyes to see, you need vision."

Hidden Shallows

In this chapter I've mentioned that people often have stories, skills or knowledge that you could never guess. These are often referred to as 'hidden depths'. What seems to rarely, if ever, get mentioned is the opposite phenomenon of 'hidden shallows'. I'm referring to cases where you tend to assume people *do* have skills, knowledge or expertise that they turn out *not* to have.

I'm a good example (and the only one I can discuss without annoying or offending anyone). It is a fact that I have an honours degree in English Literature from Sheffield University. It's a real degree. I sat the exams, dressed up in a silly hat for the graduation ceremony and still have the certificate in a box somewhere (probably). You might therefore suppose I know a thing or two about English Literature and famous books and plays. I don't. At the time I got this degree, I neither knew nor cared about literature and I still don't. During my so-called 'educational' years, all I learned was how to jump through the hoops sufficiently well to pass exams. This is quite different from actually knowing anything about the subject(s) involved.

Dictionary Corner

At the end of the 'Introduction', in the DUCK, I included a version of my life story that was intended to be mildly amusing ('About Me: Version #2'). In this fictional account, I mentioned a tense encounter with a wolf and used the term 'vulpine adversary'. 'Vulpine' refers to a fox, not a wolf. The word I should have used is 'lupine'. I know this.

I thought I'd write 'vulpine' to see if anyone gets sufficiently excited about it to write to me to correct my 'mistake', thereby proving that they haven't read the rest of the book or, specifically, this paragraph. I also wonder if any critic or reviewer will take the bait and write something lofty and condescending such as, 'Rowland claims to be a writer yet is apparently unaware of the difference between vulpine and lupine'.

Won't it be fun if this actually happens?

2. Second Foundation: About Yourself

"The 'self-image' is the key to human personality and human behaviour. Change the self image and you change the personality and the behaviour."

— Maxwell Maltz

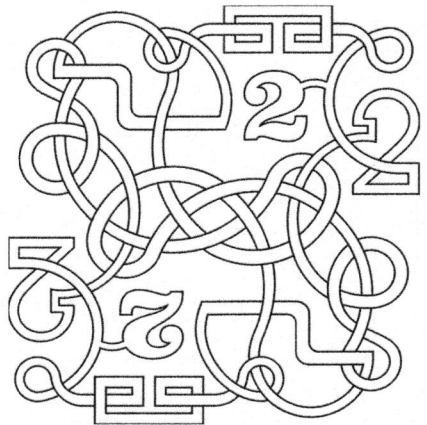

Progress Check

The first three chapters in this book cover the three foundations of People Joy:

- How you feel about yourself.

- How you feel about other people.

- How you feel about conversations.

Chapter 1 discussed how you feel about other people.

This chapter concerns your attitude towards yourself and how this affects the quality and success of the conversations you have.

Part 1: Foundations
1. About Other People
2. About Yourself
3. About Conversations

Part 2: Talking
4. Before You Talk
5. When You Talk (1)
6. When You Talk (2)
7. When You Talk (3)
8. After You Talk

Part 3: Refinements
9. The Ten-second Smile
10. Voice Magic
11. More About Other People
12. More About You
13. The Joy Of Disagreement
14. Dealing With Anger

Part 4: Special Skills
15. The Art Of Selling
16. The Art Of Persuasion
17. The Art Of Cold Reading
18. Love Is What Works

A Greatness Shared

The second foundation of People Joy is to approach conversations with this attitude:

It's great to be me and I expect it's great to be you too.

I'm not suggesting you say this out loud (unless you want to get some strange looks). Say this *to yourself*, in your inner voice, as a way to prime yourself for the conversation.

This raises an obvious question: what if you *don't* actually feel that it's great to be you? If this is the case, let me see if I can help you reach a point where you practise self-greatness every day.

Practising Self-greatness

Let's say you're ready to accept what I wrote in Chapter 1. You appreciate that people are fascinating and full of treasure waiting to be discovered. When you meet someone, you're ready to let them sense your delight in meeting them, your interest, respect and love. It might still be the case that you have a rather flat conversation that's neither enjoyable nor productive. Why? The usual reason is because, in metaphorical terms, you're not providing enough battery power.

Let me explain. In this book, I'm going to suggest you practise self-greatness, which I'll define more fully in the next section. Your sense of self-greatness is the battery power for the conversations you have. It provides the energy and light that characterise really great, happy and successful conversations. When your self-greatness is low, it's not surprising if the conversations don't glow very much.

Maybe there are reasons why your sense of self-greatness isn't, or never has been, very high. If this is an issue for you, it may be a good idea for you to seek the help of a qualified professional therapist. In recent years, I've met two excellent therapists through my work. They are James Mallinson and Annette Rainbow (that's actually her real name!). Like all the other people I mention in this book, you can find their details on my website (ianrowland.com/peoplejoy).

The suggestions in this chapter are intended for people who do *not* need the services of a professional therapist.

Realising Your Greatness

In People Joy terms, to practise self-greatness means to be free from self-doubt, fear and conflict.

I strongly and emphatically believe that everyone should practise self-greatness every day. I believe the best way to go through life is to know that you're great which, in turn, helps you to appreciate *the greatness in others*. This makes a transformative difference to the conversations you have. I am opposed to anything that undermines or detracts from anyone's sense of self-greatness.

Please note this important distinction: I am not suggesting you *believe* you're great. I'm suggesting your *realise* you are.

You may believe that in order to be a 'great' person, you have to do something dramatic such as win a gold medal or be a movie star. This is not the case. You're great because every day you do something difficult and admirable: you try to live your life. Like everyone else, you're trying to get through life as best you can. Every day, you try to move away from things that feel bad and towards things that feel good. This is what *everyone* is doing, all the time, and it isn't easy. Life can be hard, tough and challenging. You have to deal with whatever physical and mental limitations you have. You also have to deal with rotten luck, setbacks, loss, failure, unfairness, disappointment and (sometimes) tragedy. Given that you have to deal with all these challenges from time to time, if you're managing to live your life then you're entitled to know that you're great. The only condition is that you have to embrace three good ideas:

- Don't hurt yourself.

- Don't hurt anyone else.

- Be kind, be helpful and have fun if you can.

All human experience to date suggests that these ideas work better than anything else we've tried (such as hating and hurting). Provided you respect these ideas, you're entitled to embrace, enjoy and share your self-greatness.

If you still don't feel that you're great, this is probably because you haven't yet obtained your freedom set. Let me see if I can help you.

Your Freedom Set

To practise self-greatness means being free from three problems:

- Self-doubt.

- Fear.

- Conflict (with people in your life).

These three problems are cold, icy chains that diminish the shine of your life. I suggest you try to break free from these chains and be your own Freedom Hero. If you've been through emotional trauma, this will be far from easy. Nonetheless, I believe it's worth the effort. You're entitled to these freedoms and deserve no less

I'm going to look at each of these problems in turn and offer some suggestions you might find helpful.

Freedom From Self-Doubt

Many people are troubled by self-doubt to some extent. This can take many different forms and can also vary according to context. You might feel relaxed and confident in some situations but plagued by self-doubt in others. Self-doubt is seriously bad news. It harms your mental, emotional and physical health and also gives rise to stress. It's therefore a good idea to aim to free yourself from self-doubt entirely.

I do not mean to be glib about this. As I mentioned above, I know that some people suffer from self-doubt because they have been through emotionally traumatic experiences. This is unfortunate and I know that recovery can take a long time. In this section, I want to explore three common sources of self-doubt and some effective ways of dealing with them. They are:

- The emotional legacy of failure.

- Stinging criticism.

- Conparing (I'll explain this term when we get to it).

Let's take a look at these problems and possible fixes.

The Emotional Legacy Of Failure

You have almost certainly had the experience of trying to do something and failing. For example, it's quite common for this to happen during your school days. You attempt to do something, fail and then get mocked either by other children or a teacher. Similar things can happen at other times of your life as well.

When you go through an experience like this, you can sometimes shrug it off. However, on other occasions, you might feel a sense of hurt, shame or humiliation. You might store this emotional experience of failure inside yourself as a negative message that says, 'I'm not good enough', or, 'I'm not as good as the others'. This feeling can persist for years or decades after the original incident.

What's The Fix?

See if this helps. When you came into this world, you didn't sign a contract saying you would always succeed. There is therefore no reason to hold yourself to this standard. No one else has any right to hold you to this standard either. You never agreed or promised to succeed all the time.

'Failing' is just a clumsy word people use when they mean 'learning'. As you go through life, you can try to achieve things or not try. If you never try, you'll never experience failure but you'll never experience success either. As people say, 'The person who never made a mistake never made anything.'

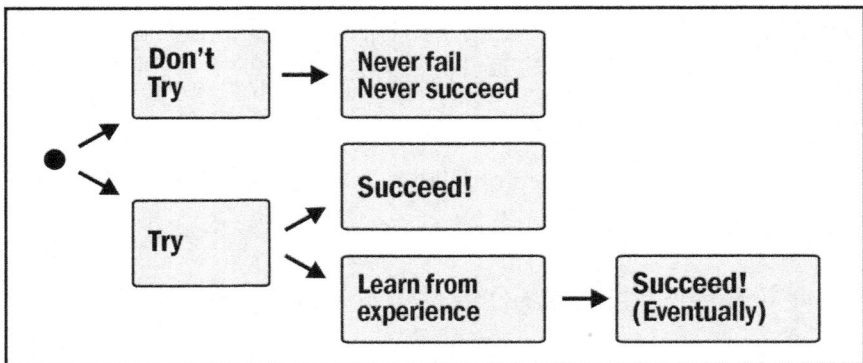

When you *try* to do something, you will either succeed or fail. If you succeed, well done! If you fail, you will learn from the experience so you'll do better next time. Experience is the greatest teacher and learning from experience is how you eventually succeed.

- Try or not try.

- Succeed or learn.

This is all you can do in life. This is all *anyone* can do! This is what everyone on the planet is doing, day after day.

The Comedian's Tale

I once had a friend who was just starting out as a stand-up comedian. One evening, I went to see her perform at a 'try out' gig. She did her ten minutes and, to be honest, she wasn't very good. As she came off stage, someone made a harsh, scathing remark to the effect that she was rubbish and should give up. My friend didn't feel at all hurt or upset. Why not? Because here's what she *could* have said:

"You're right. I didn't do well this evening. But at least I tried. Stand-up comedy is really hard. It takes a long time to learn how to do it well. So, this is what I'm doing. I'm trying and learning from each experience so that one day I'll be good. If you think there's a better way to achieve my goals, by all means tell me what it is. All you've done is sit in a chair and say something unkind. That's *easy*. At least I was up there, trying and learning how to do something difficult."

My friend didn't actually *say* this out loud, which would have been unnecessarily defensive and argumentative. But it's what she *thought* to herself. All performers and entertainers have the same outlook. You want to hurl abuse? Go ahead. At least we're up there trying.

Failing just means learning. Learning leads to success (eventually). What if you keep trying and keep failing? I suggest you read about people you regard as successful. In almost *every* case, you'll find they failed a thousand times before they were successful. It takes a while.

The 'Until Sleep' Rule

While you may know on a *rational* level that trying and learning is all you can do, it's not always *easy* to handle failure *emotionally*. There will be times when it's a bitter experience.

If you're ever in this situation, I suggest you follow the Until Sleep rule. Allow yourself to feel bad for one evening *until you go to sleep*. You can feel sorry for yourself, moan to your partner or a friend and sulk a bit until you go to bed. Give yourself this much time to process how you feel and come to terms with the experience. When you wake up the next morning, have a big stretch. Enjoy and embrace the new day and the start of the rest of your life.

Progress Check

We're looking at three sources of self-doubt. The first one was:

- The emotional experience of failure.

Now let's look at the second one.

2. Stinging Criticism

As you make your way through life, there will be times when people criticise you or your work. In some cases, you might not care what they say. In other cases, the criticism can sting, hurt your feelings or make you wonder whether you should carry on trying.

What's The Fix?

I think it helps to remember that 'criticism' can mean two different things. It sometimes just means someone's opinion about whether or not they like something. This has nothing to do with *merit*. I once knew a classical musician who said he disliked Mozart's music. He wasn't saying it lacked merit. He was just saying he didn't *like* it. The next time you fail to please all the people, all the time, remember that you're in the same category as Mozart!

Everyone is entitled to their opinion about whether or not they *like* something. Some people will like this book and some won't. This meaning of 'criticism' doesn't generally cause feelings of self-doubt.

The second meaning of 'criticism' involves *judgment* about whether or not something has any *merit*. When people say your work isn't any good or lacks merit, these words can hurt a little and dent your confidence. Fortunately, I can give you a perfect way to remove this sting forever. Whenever someone criticises you in this way, simply ask yourself if their criticism passes two tests:

- Is it *informed?* Do they know what they are talking about?

- Is it *constructive?* Do they want to help you to improve and to do better next time?

If criticism passes these two tests then you should *welcome* it because it's extremely helpful. Whoever the critic is, buy them a cup of coffee, listen to them and take notes. They're giving you free advice and expertise that will help you to improve. Make the most of it!

If the criticism fails either or both of these tests, then it's just useless, like wet confetti or a concrete trampoline. There's simply nothing you can do with it. This being the case, you can safely ignore it. You don't have to get angry, defensive or argumentative. Just smile, thank the critic and get on with your day.

Progress Check

We're looking at three sources of self-doubt. The first two were:

- The emotional experience of failure.

- Stinging criticism.

Now let's look at the third and final one.

3. Conparing

'Conpare' isn't a real word. I made it up. It means to *con* yourself, and hurt your own feelings, by comparing yourself unfavourably to someone or something else.

The world offers you countless opportunities to conpare yourself to someone else and conclude that you're inadequate in some way. Doing this undermines your self-greatness. It's not a good idea.

What's The Fix?

You can completely insulate yourself from the harm of conparison. All you have to do is remind yourself of two points.

First of all, just because there's an *opportunity* to conpare yourself doesn't mean you have to take it. Every day, you have the opportunity to pick up a spoon and whack yourself over the head with it. This would probably hurt a bit. Fortunately, you don't need to *take* this opportunity. You can decline it. It's the same with any opportunity to compare (or conpare) your self to someone else — perhaps because they seem more beautiful, successful or popular. Simply because the *opportunity* is there doesn't mean you have to *take* it. As with the spoon, it won't achieve anything and might hurt a bit.

Secondly, reality is a good place to live. In fact, it's better than any alternative. If conparing is the sickness, reality is the soothing, healing, cure-all medicine you need.

Let's apply these points to three familiar types of conparison.

Badvertising. This is my term for advertising that tries to make you feel bad about yourself. All badvertising says you're not quite good enough the way you are but you *could* be if you buy Product X. Badvertising preys on insecurities and self-doubt.

Not all advertising works this way. Some ads just offer information: 'We sell a good range of sofas and we have a sale on this weekend'. There's nothing wrong with this. However, there is quite a lot of badvertising around and in my opinion it's despicable. I know the people who make these ads might say they are *empowering* consumers and helping them to satisfy their aspirations. This debate can get complicated. I'm just opposed to anything that causes people to feel inadequate or that undermines their self-greatness.

First of all, you can decline the opportunity to conpare yourself to the photos in the ads. You can choose not to be brainwashed by toxic trash that wants you to doubt yourself.

Secondly, apply the reality check. Badvertising images are calculated, predatory pretzel fictions that have nothing to do with reality. Consider a cosmetics advert featuring an elegant, glamorous model with sun-kissed, flawless skin. In some (not all) adverts of this type, the implication is that if you don't look like the model in the photo then you're not quite good enough. However, even the model *herself* doesn't look like that in real life! That glossy photo is what you get when you take someone with good genes whose full-time job is to look good, sit her down in a photographic studio, let a professional team of make-up artists and stylists do their thing, adjust the lighting until the end of time, take eleventy gazillion photos, choose the best one and use a little digital 'enhancement' here and there.

Whatever they're selling won't make you look like that model unless it can give you her genes and her life. Luckily, there's absolutely no need to look like her. Just looking like you is absolutely fine. Whatever your face happens to look like, at least it has the merit of being real.

Social Media Smugness. Here's a second type of conparison. Suppose you're browsing social media one day. You see a smug young couple boasting about having bought their first house. "We're both under thirty", they say, "yet we've just bought this wonderful three-bedroom house. What have *you* achieved?"

First of all, this is an *opportunity* to conpare your life to theirs. You don't have to take it any more than you need to whack yourself on the head with a spoon. Secondly, here comes the reality check. For all you know, the entire article or video might be fake. Even if those people *have* recently acquired a nice house, so what? Maybe they just have wealthy parents who bought the house for them.

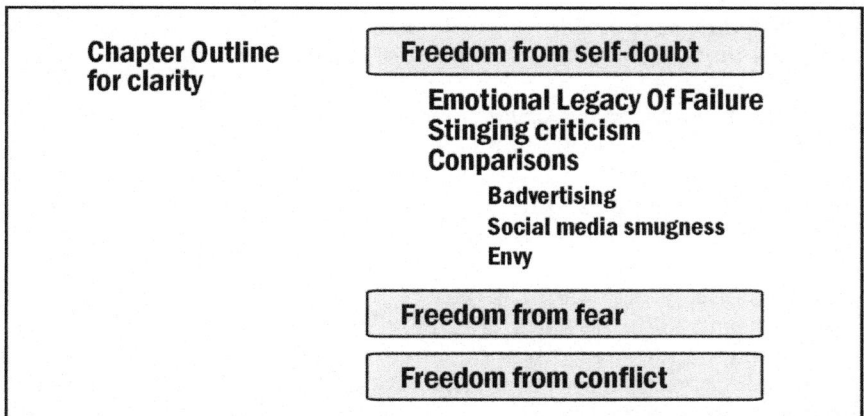

Chapter Outline for clarity	**Freedom from self-doubt**
	Emotional Legacy Of Failure **Stinging criticism** **Conparisons** **Badvertising** **Social media smugness** **Envy**
	Freedom from fear
	Freedom from conflict

Envy. The third and final example (of typical conparisons) involves simple human envy. 'He's more handsome than I am and earns more and drives a nicer car'. 'She always looks amazing and she's a Director where she works and has at least four holidays a year'.

The same two steps apply. First of all, the fact that you *can* make this type of comparison doesn't mean you *have* to. Secondly, let's choose to live in reality. Everyone's doing the best they can with what they've got. This isn't *easy* because life's a challenge and often unfair. If you knew everything about Mr. Handsome, you'd realise he has his share of worries and problems. It's true they may be *different* problems from yours but they are problems nonetheless. The same goes for Miss Beautiful Top Executive.

We can focus on our differences and live our lives for ourselves. Or, we can focus on the ways in which we're all alike, with our respective problems and struggles, and choose to help one another. The first way doesn't work. The second way does. Love is what works.

I hope this trio of examples (badvertising, social media smugness, envy) has made the point: you never need to conpare yourself to anyone or anything. Decline the opportunity. Choose reality.

When Doubt Is Good

Are there times when self-doubt is good? Yes.

In this section, I'm referring to self-doubt that undermines your belief in your *value* as a person, your *abilities* and your *potential*. The type of doubt that corrodes your sense of self-greatness.

Doubt is good when it's *protective*. If you're walking around near the edge of a tall cliff, I don't want you to have *reckless* confidence that you'll be safe even if you get very close to the edge. I'd prefer you to have some healthy doubts about this and to take a few sensible precautions for your own safety.

Doubt is also good when it's part of honest intellectual enquiry. I'm not suggesting you go through life with an arrogant attitude, always convinced that you're right about everything. Be willing to doubt what you think you know and to change your views if someone gives you a good reason to do so.

Progress Check

We're looking at freedom from three chains: self-doubt, fear and conflict. We've just looked at three common causes of self-doubt (failure, criticism and conparisons) and ways to overcome them.

Now let's move on the second type of highly desirable freedom.

Freedom From Fear

Fear never adds to life. It only subtracts from it. This being so, I believe you should aim to go through life with as little fear as possible — and preferably none at all.

I know it isn't always easy to escape fear. There may be circumstances in which you feel afraid of someone or something and can't do much about it. If this is the case, you have my heartfelt sympathy and I can only hope you get the help you need. This section is not about these situations. It's about the type of situation where you *can* do something to alleviate or remove the fear you feel.

Whenever you experience fear, ask yourself if feeling afraid is the *best* choice you can make at this moment. Would it be better to calm down and consider your options? For example, you could choose to go into problem-solving mode. (There's a section all about this in Chapter 3.) This will help you to decide the best course of action to take. Taking action doesn't *guarantee* you'll overcome whatever is causing the fear but it gives you a *chance* to do so.

Another good idea is to realise how destructive fears arise. You are imagining a bad thing happening (at some point in the near or distant future) and then feeling afraid of the experience and its consequences. In effect, you are fearing *your own imagination*. You don't need to do this. You *own* your imagination. You are the projectionist in this particular cinema or movie theatre. You can project whatever you want on to your imagination screen. I suggest you fill the screen with positive images, not fearful ones.

Scenario: you are going for a job interview. You look ahead and worry about being nervous, giving stupid answers and making a mess of it. These fears tend to be self-fulfilling. Your fears give rise to worry and anxiety that make it likely you'll perform badly at the interview. You don't need to sabotage your prospects in this way. Step one: ask yourself if fear is really your best option. Step two: say 'nothing bad will happen' and take control of your imagination screen. Visualise the entire interview going superbly well!

Have done with fear. Don't let it get in the way of loving your life, future and potential. I'm not saying this is easy. I am saying you can at least work towards the goal of a life without fear. While it may take time and you may need some help, I believe you can get there.

Freedom From Conflict

Here's the third and final part of practising self-greatness: as far as you can, eliminate conflict from your life. Is this easier said than done? Yes. Is it worth doing? Certainly.

Are there family members you've fallen out with so you never speak to them? Try to get back on speaking terms and rebuild the relationship. Fallen out with a neighbour? Actively try to rebuild the neighbourly relationship. Had a good friend that you fell out with for some reason? See if you can be on friendly terms once again.

None of this is easy to do. In some cases, it might be exceptionally difficult. Try anyway — always provided it is *safe* to do so and you aren't exposing yourself to the risk of harm. You will have to be humble. You will have to abandon the attitude that says you were right and they were wrong. You will have to swallow your pride and be magnanimous and accommodating. Egotism is a bad driver to leave in charge of the limousine of your life: can't steer, usually drunk, hopeless at navigation. It will drive you into walls, ditches and rivers on a regular basis.

Do your best to reach the point where there are no conflicts or strained relationships in your life. The person you get back in touch with doesn't have to become your best friend or closest relationship. The point is to eliminate from your life any feelings of conflict and broken communication. I've been through this process two or three times and I know it's not easy. Nonetheless, it's possible.

Choose the ability to make positive changes in your life — such as going from a broken relationship to communication. If you can't quite get to friendship, at least aim for a cordial peace.

The Purpose Of Self-Greatness

Practising self-greatness is not about being arrogant and always thinking you're right. It's not about being a loud, self-centred, attention-seeking egomaniac. It doesn't mean talking about yourself all the time or thinking that you're high status and everyone else is low status. Self-greatness means you practise being kind and loving towards yourself so you get better at being kind and loving towards others. It means being someone that other people warm to and like. It's about practising seeing the greatness in yourself so you're better at seeing and appreciating it in others.

When you achieve the freedoms I mentioned in this chapter, people can sense the warmth and respond to it. On a subtle and instinctive level, they sense in you the absence of self-doubt, fear and conflict and feel they'd like to enjoy the same freedoms. In some cases, you may be able to help them to do so.

Chapter Summary

This chapter was about how you feel about yourself. I suggested that you should practise self-greatness and try to free yourself from three cold, icy chains of self-limitation. The main headings were:

- A greatness shared.

- Practising self-greatness.

- Your freedom set.

- Freedom from self-doubt.

- Freedom from fear.

- Freedom from conflict.

This completes the second foundational chapter of People Joy, addressing how you feel about yourself and how this affects the conversations you have. The next chapter concerns how you feel about conversations in general.

DUCK

Solzhenitsyn Quote

Part of this chapter referred to feelings of envy. In his book 'The Gulag Archipelago', Aleksandr Solzhenitsyn wrote, "Our envy of others devours us most of all." This is part of a longer passage that I can't reproduce here because it's copyright. However, you should be able to find it online fairly easily. The passage I'm referring to begins, "What about the main thing in life, all its riddles? If you want, I'll spell it out for you right now."

I strongly recommend that you take a moment to read this incredibly moving and inspirational passage. It's certainly thought-provoking and says a great deal in relatively few words.

Cuckoo's Nest

In this chapter I mentioned that you should always feel proud of yourself for *trying* even if you don't get the result you wanted. As I'm sure many of you will know, this point is exceptionally well illustrated in the glorious 1975 film 'One Flew Over The Cuckoo's Nest', starring Jack Nicholson. I won't include any spoilers here. If you're familiar with the film, you probably know the scene I'm referring to. If you don't know the film, may I suggest you watch it at your earliest convenience. I first saw this film in my teens and it transformed how I felt about trying and failing. I'm sure many other fans of the film would say the same.

The film is based on Ken Kesey's 1962 novel of the same name. This is about as brilliant as a novel can be and I highly recommend it.

A Good New Word

Earlier in this chapter, I wrote, "If you struggle to accept that you're great…". When I was writing this bit, I initially mis-typed the word 'struggle' as 'sturggle'. First of all, I appreciated the delicious irony of having struggled to correctly type the word 'struggle'. I fear that I only narrowly missed being sucked into some strange, endless loop of self-referential failure and clumsiness.

Secondly, I have to say that I like the look of the word 'sturggle'. It suggests the letters *struggling* to get themselves in the correct order. What could be more appropriate? I hope this new word will catch on. However, it might be difficult to persuade everyone to adopt it. It could be a bit of an uphill sturggle. (Ta-dum! Punchline!)

Black Box Thinking

Part of this chapter was about modifying one's attitude towards failure. If you're interested in this subject, I recommend Matthew Syed's wonderful book, 'Black Box Thinking'. Among other things, it explains why we should all develop a much more positive attitude towards so-called failure.

Even if you do nothing else, read the first chapter of this book. It will change your life and you will never worry about 'failure' ever again. You will realise that *every* great invention, from the steam engine to the smartphone, was the result of a long process of research that involved lots and lots of *failing*. This is why some people use the acronym 'FAIL' to mean 'First Adventure In Learning'.

3. Third Foundation: About Conversations

"Remaining open to the powers of conversation – to new evidence and better arguments – is not only essential for rationality. It is essential for love."

— *Sam Harris*

Progress Check

This part of the book is about the three foundations of People Joy.

Foundation 1 addressed how you feel about other people. I suggested you should see people as utterly, endlessly, beautifully fascinating.

Foundation 2 addressed how you feel about yourself. I suggested you should practise self-greatness (which in turn will help you to see the greatness in others).

Now let's look at the third People Joy foundation: how you feel about conversations in general.

Part 1: Foundations

1. **About Other People**
2. **About Yourself**
3. **About Conversations**

Part 2: Talking

4. Before You Talk
5. When You Talk (1)
6. When You Talk (2)
7. When You Talk (3)
8. After You Talk

Part 3: Refinements

9. The Ten-second Smile
10. Voice Magic
11. More About Other People
12. More About You
13. The Joy Of Disagreement
14. Dealing With Anger

Part 4: Special Skills

15. The Art Of Selling
16. The Art Of Persuasion
17. The Art Of Cold Reading
18. Love Is What Works

A Chance To Win

The third foundation of People Joy is this:

Every conversation is a chance to win.

Most people have conversations that are *passive* and that lack any *intention*. The People Joy approach is to have conversations that are *active* and *intentional*.

An *active* conversation means that you keep your mind switched on rather than relying on autopilot. It means you stay aware and mindful of the conversation's potential and interested in what it could lead to. Active conversations involve a *bit* more work and mental energy than passive ones. However, on the positive side, they deliver much greater results and rewards.

As for having *intentional* conversations, you should always *intend* to *achieve a win*. A 'win' means one of these three goals:

- Enjoy a mind walk (which we looked at in Chapter 1).

- Achieve something positive.

- Build a connection.

Let's take a look at each of these.

Enjoy A Mind Walk

I covered this in Chapter 1 but I'm including it here for completeness. Every time you talk to someone and go for a mind walk, you can award yourself a win. You have found someone fascinating, given them some time and attention and taken an interest in their story. You have (almost certainly) learned about some aspect of their life that's surprising and that you would never have guessed.

Well done! This is a hugely productive way to talk to people and very much in the spirit of People Joy. Plus you get to discover all sorts of treasure and enjoy a wealth of free entertainment!

Achieve Something Positive

Every conversation is an opportunity to achieve something positive. This positive result can take different forms, according to context. Here are a few ideas.

Perhaps you can brighten the day of the other person (OP) just by smiling and being cheerful. You might be the only person all day who makes them feel acknowledged, seen and appreciated.

If the OP is clearly over-worked, perhaps you can be the one person who *isn't* barking at them to get ten things done at once. You can be the patient presence who says something like, "I can see you're busy. Take your time. I can come back later if you like."

If the OP is in a good mood, perhaps you can find out why, share the moment and offer your congratulations, respect and admiration. When people have good news, they like to share it with someone.

If the OP looks stressed, maybe you can help (provided this is *welcome* and *not intrusive*). You can often bring some light into the world just by being a good listener. As Shakespeare puts it:

> *"Oft times our best expression's well confined*
> *To silenced true regard for what we hear*
> *The patient witness renders service kind*
> *To souls that bear the scar of private tear"*
>   (Troilus And Cressida, Act III, scene ii)

If the OP has a problem, and wants some help, maybe you can go into problem-solving mode and work on it together. There's a section about solving problems later in this chapter.

A lot of people take care of routine tasks and never get thanked or credited. Maybe you can offer a bit of validation or gratitude that they'll enjoy. "I know working out the rota for the shop floor *every* week is a difficult job but you do it really well, so thanks."

Can you be a positive presence in the OP's life, and brighten their day, by saying something playful, funny or humorous? I do this a lot but it's not the right approach for everyone. (See the later chapter devoted to 'The Ten-second Smile'.)

Maybe you can offer the OP a simple, honest compliment. You could say something nice about their skill, dependability, appearance, sense of humour, the way they handled a situation or something else. There are three golden rules: the compliment must be *sincere, selfless* (not motivated by personal gain) and *welcome*.

This is not an exhaustive list. There are many other ways to achieve something positive when you talk to someone. All you have to do is find *one*. Relish the challenge and enjoy the achievement.

A note about compliments: if you're a man talking to a woman, please be sensitive. Never offer compliments that she'll regard as creepy or make her feel unsafe. Don't sound like you're trying to 'chat her up' or 'hit on her' unless this is *clearly* appropriate and welcome from *her* point of view. If she's annoyed by what you said, you should just apologise, go away and leave her alone.

Build A Connection

In this section, we're looking at three different ways to achieve a 'win' during a conversation. We've covered two so far: enjoy a mind walk and achieve something positive. The third type of win is simply this: you manage to build a good connection.

Every time you meet someone, for example through mutual friends or at a work event, you have a choice. You can either have a bland and perfunctory chat, after which you forget about one another's existence, or you can build an enduring connection. You won't *always* want to build a connection, of course. However, if you *do* then you can count this as a win in People Joy terms.

I often make good connections with random strangers I meet, say, on a train, in a cafe, in a store or while enjoying a walk in the park. Obviously, whether this is possible and appropriate will depend on the prevailing social codes in your part of the world. However, in cases where it *is* possible, I think it's a wonderful thing to turn a random stranger into one of your contacts and, later, maybe even a friend. The advent of smartphones and social media has made it easier than ever before to keep in touch with people you meet. There might come a time when it's useful for the other person to know how to reach you (with all your knowledge, skills and contacts) or vice versa. You never can tell how things will work out!

There's no *downside* to having a wide social circle and knowing lots of people. If I know a couple of hundred people, all with their various skills, talents and knowledge, I have a couple of hundred potential sources of help when problems arise. It also means I have a few hundred opportunities to be helpful to other people. This is another 'win', because being useful feels great and fulfilling.

I'd like to add a couple of points about helping people.

I've heard it said that givers need to know how to set limits because takers never do. I haven't often met this problem but it may be something to consider. It's all right to set boundaries if the need arises. Sometimes, you need to be clear that *you* decide how much you're going to help other people. It's your choice.

You also have to strike the right balance between how much of your time you devote to you and how much you devote to the rest of the world. There's time for giving and time for living. Superman helps a *lot* of people... but still has his Fortress of Solitude.

The Merits Of Intention

Choosing to have *active* and *intentional* conversations delivers many benefits. It can also help people who suffer from a degree of social anxiety or a lack of social confidence. When people are trying to learn new social skills, they often wonder *what* to talk about during a conversation. They worry about coming across as boring if they just rely on stale topics such as the weather (often seen as a conversational cliché here in the UK). They may also worry about how to start a conversation or about running out of things to say.

Here's my suggestion. Rather than wondering *what* to say, focus instead on your *intention,* as explained in this chapter. When you have a clear intention, in the majority of cases you'll find the words follow fairly easily. Intention provides invention.

Problem-solving Mode (PERMIT)

I mentioned that you might sometimes want to go into problem-solving mode. As this point is going to come up a few times in this book, let me offer a few notes about solving problems.

When a problem arises, you can respond in two ways: *emotionally* or *methodically*. They're both good options for different reasons. It's all right to respond emotionally *if* you can do so safely and you need the release. Some people have to go through this stage *before* they can settle down and start approaching the problem methodically. Other people can reach the methodical stage straight away.

Here's the methodical approach.

1. What square am I on? Start from a clear picture of the current situation.

2. What square do I want to get to? Be clear about the solution(s) you want or would find acceptable. It's hard to aim correctly if you haven't decided on a target.

3. What are my options — the different courses of action I could take? And what are the pros and cons of each of these candidate options?

4. Having assessed the pros and cons, what's the *best* option?

When you're evaluating possible courses of action, you might like to use PERMIT analysis. It's not hard. Solving problems usually involves one or more of these elements:

People / **E**xpertise / **R**esources / **M**oney / **I**nformation / **T**ime

These are easy to remember as 'PERMIT'.

'Expertise' also covers experience. It's the 'know how' part of the formula, such as knowing how to use a piece of software, translate from French to Chinese or drive a fork-lift truck.

'Resources' in this case refers to materials, tools, equipment and supplies you might need, such as timber, a garden rake or a sheet metal joddler flanger. (This is a real thing.)

Consider which of these PERMIT elements you need.

If you need something and can get it, good.

If you don't have it, and can't get it, ask yourself whether this is a temporary situation, which might change, or permanent. If it's permanent, you have to do without that item and come up with an alternative plan or workaround.

Sometimes, you might want resources that costs money. If you have the money you need, all is well. If you don't, you have to use an alternative to money. This means having to barter with the supplier, for example by offering your expertise or labour in return for what you want. If none of these options are practical, your final option is to ask the supplier for a favour. The more you practise People Joy, the more likely they are to agree.

If you need to barter, be honest, likeable and reasonable. Don't start from the position of wondering if you can or cannot achieve a deal. Assume that you *can* and you just have to find out *how*. See the picture from the other person's point of view to appreciate why they may or may not want to do a deal with you. (The later chapter on persuasion will help.)

When you start working on the problem, track your progress and remain flexible. In the military, they say 'no plan survives contact with the enemy'. You may have to revise your plan as events unfold and new information comes to light. Sometimes, you may even have to start all over again.

Using this methodical approach, you'll be able to solve 95% of life's problems, particularly if you practise People Joy.

The 5% of problems you *can't* solve are part of everyone's journey through life. This is a good time to remember the Serenity Key: 'Change what you can't accept and accept what you can't change'. Welcome the learning opportunity. Welcome the chance to mature as a person and realise you can't always get what you want. Also, remain aware and mindful of all the problems in life that other people have to deal with but you don't.

The 'How Can I?' Twist

This is a little problem-solving trick that all therapists and counsellors know about and use in their work.

Your brain tries to answer whichever question you ask it. If you ask yourself, 'Why can't I stop smoking?', your brain will start trying to come up with a few good answers: because you've been doing it a long time; because it's powerfully addictive; because you find it pleasurable and relaxing; because it's locked in to so many of your daily habits and routines.

However, if you ask yourself a different question, you get a different set of answers. If you ask, 'How can I stop smoking?', your brain might say: try hypnotherapy; try patches and nicotine substitutes; talk to friends who have managed to quit and ask them how they did it; consult them; start changing some of your daily habits and routines.

You see the difference? It works the same way with, for example, a team meeting at work. If you ask everyone, 'Why can't we process orders more quickly?', they'll come up with reasons why this can't be done. If you change the question to, 'How can...', your team will possibly start suggesting ways to make improvements.

When you change the question, you change the answers. Try switching from 'Why can't I...?' mode to 'How can I...?' mode.

On Solving Problems

When you're trying to solve a problem, here's something to bear in mind. Scientists say the human brain is the most complex thing in the known universe. It's basically a squishy problem-solving machine. Solving problems is what it does and what it's superbly good at. Take a moment to consider some of the human brain's finest achievements and greatest triumphs.

A human brain managed to produce Emily Brontë's 'Wuthering Heights', vaccines and antibiotics, the Hoover dam, Bach's Allegro BWV 998, powered flight, algebra, the process for converting grapes into wine, Pink Floyd's 'Dark Side Of The Moon', geo-stationary satellites and the 'Germans' episode of 'Fawlty Towers'.

It also gave us the Great Pyramid of Giza, holograms, Keith Jarrett's 'Koln Concert', Truman Capote's 'A Christmas Memory', katsu curry sauce, Cantor's diagonal proof of infinite sets, Gaudi's Sagrada Família, Sting's 'Fields Of Gold' (and all his other songs for that matter), the internet, Virginia Woolf's 'Orlando', the Sistine Chapel ceiling, Stevie Wonder's 'Songs In The Key Of Life', the Ruyi Bridge, deep-space telescopes, CT scans, Christine McVie's 'Songbird', Bill Forysth's film 'Local Hero', the Hagia Sophia Grand Mosque, the songs of Cole Porter and 'Catch-22' by Joseph Heller (the greatest novel of the 20th century).

All these things started off as ideas in a human brain (or several human brains). What's more, human brains solved all the problems involved in transforming these ideas into real things. You've got a human brain sitting between your ears right now. It's ready to solve whatever problems you care to feed into it.

In fact, your brain is doing something utterly remarkable *at this very moment*. It is performing a *vast* amount of computation to take some squiggly black marks and shapes, called letters and words, and extract *meaning* from them. The marks and shapes have no intrinsic meaning whatsoever (as becomes obvious when you see a foreign language that uses a completely different set of squiggles). You had to learn the extremely complicated process of linking the scribbles and squiggles with sounds, words, things and ideas. Yet your brain now does this so quickly and so well that, until I happened to mention it, you weren't even aware of this process and just took it for granted!

By the way, if you don't like my list of the human brain's impressive achievements, feel free to substitute your own examples. However, I have to insist that 'Catch-22' stays on the list. If you disagree then, sorry, but we can't be friends. I know this isn't a very People Joy attitude but even I have my boundaries.

Attentive Energy And Emotional Labour

Just before ending this chapter, I'd like to mention two more aspects of the value of conversations. My friend Katrina Kroetch is a highly successful magician from Los Angeles. She told me she uses the term 'attentive energy' to refer to any situation where someone gives their time and attention to someone else in a way that's welcome and may serve a therapeutic purpose.

This can take many forms. Clearly, therapists offer attentive energy to their clients by definition. However, other people do it too. Examples would include a teacher spending extra time with a youngster who's struggling, a barman sympathising with a customer drowning his sorrows or a tarot reader giving someone a reading (as we'll discuss in Chapter 17). I like the term 'attentive energy'. I think a large part of People Joy can be seen as relishing opportunities to offer attentive energy to other people, wherever it's welcome and appropriate.

Katrina also told me about Arlie Hochschild, who coined the term 'emotional labour'. This refers to the effort required to manage and maintain relationships, in the home, in the workplace or elsewhere, that many women do all the time and that most men do *not* do.

Consider a team working in a typical office. Everyone makes their contribution (one hopes) to the basic function of the team, taking care of deliverables, deadlines, schedules and so on. However, the women on the team are the ones likely to be taking care of their colleagues on an emotional level. They are the ones who will find a quiet moment to say, "You looked a bit distracted during the meeting and you were a bit short-tempered with Linda just now. It's not like you. What's the matter?" Women do this at home, at work, on social occasions and in many other contexts as well. It's not just about expressing concern but also doing the work to address whatever issues need to be addressed.

Inaccurate gender stereotypes don't help anyone. One cannot say that all women are one thing and all men are another. It's true that some men perform emotional labour and some women don't. Nonetheless, it's fair to say that *most* of this work is performed by women. (There are reasons for this which I won't go into here.) The corollary is that it's mostly women who get the sense of *fulfilment* that comes from doing this type of work. I think part of People Joy can be seen as encouraging us all, especially men, to perform emotional labour. This would be greatly to *everyone's* advantage.

The Conversational Butterfly Effect

'The Butterfly Effect', as I expect you know, refers to the way small and seemingly trivial events can have unpredictable and significant consequences. This phenomenon provides another reason to place great value on every chance to have a conversation. When you meet someone and get to know them, you never know what that connection might lead to in the future. It's impossible to anticipate what the consequences might be for you, for them or for other people you already know.

Not long ago, a friend of mine had a question about the world of dance and dancing. I was able to put her in touch with Joan, in Las Vegas, a magician who also knows everything there is to know about dancing. (The answer, if you're curious, was 'The Lindy Hop'.) How do I know Joan? About 20 years ago I was in Vegas and met up with Bob, who took me to a bar on the outskirts of town frequented by magicians and like-minded souls. Joan happened to be there. How did I know Bob? Through the magic world and because he'd read my first book on cold reading. How did I come to write that book? Partly because when I was still a teenager I had a conversation with my friend David and he mentioned cold reading. A conversation I had in my teens meant that about 55 years later I could help someone with a question about dancing!

I'm sure you can think of similar examples in your own life. You never know how a conversation you have with one person, on one day, might have consequences years or decades later. All the conversations you have in your life are a maze of tangled, criss-crossing threads and strange connections. To mix metaphors, every conversation causes ripples in the pond.

This is another good reason to talk to people, find out about them and make good connections. Among all the other benefits, you may often be able to do someone a favour by putting them in touch with someone you know. I think this is part of both the fun and practical value of People Joy

Chapter Summary

In this chapter, I suggested that for People Joy purposes you should approach conversations with an *active* mind (rather than a passive one) and the *intention* to *achieve a win*. The main headings were:

- A chance to win.

- Enjoy a mind walk.

- Achieve something positive.

- Build a connection.

- Problem-solving mode (PERMIT).

- Attentive energy and emotional labour.

- The conversational 'butterfly effect'.

It's always good to achieve a win! People Joy leads to victories both large and small for you and for people you meet.

DUCK

There's Always More Treasure

It can be worth going on a mind walk even when you're talking to someone you've known for a long time. There's always more treasure to be found. Here's a wonderful example.

I've known my friend Ian Kendall for about thirty years. He's a highly talented professional magician from Edinburgh who has done a few other jobs in the past. While I was writing this book, Ian happened to be down in London in order to present a lecture at The Magic Circle. We managed to find time to meet up for lunch. In the course of an extremely lively and wide-ranging conversation, I learned that in 1986 Ian had been the official Coach to the Malaysian Commonwealth Games fencing team! I was absolutely astounded to hear this. I'm pretty sure we had never even *mentioned* fencing before. How could I have known Ian for *three decades* without this *ever* coming up?

Fakespeare

In this chapter, I included four lines that I said were by Shakespeare. In fact, I made them up. They are nonsensical drivel that, if you squint a bit, look like something a bad Elizabethan poet might have scribbled on an 'off' day. I call this sort of thing 'Fakespeare'.

There are a few more bits of Fakespeare scattered throughout this book for no better reason than I felt like including them. Whenever you see me 'quote' a few lines and attribute them to Shakespeare, they aren't really by him. However, I'd love to see the day when one of these bits of Fakespeare gets picked up and quoted somewhere as if it's genuine. Stranger things have happened.

I like to take existing bits of text, or famous speeches, and create the Fakespeare equivalent. For example, here are a few lines taken from the instruction manual for an Indesit washing machine:

'To pause the wash cycle in progress, press this button: the corresponding indicator light will flash orange, while the indicator light for the current wash cycle phase will remain lit in a fixed manner. If the 'Door Locked' indicator light is switched off, the door may be opened. To start the wash cycle from the point at which it was interrupted, press this button again.'

Here's my Fakespeare version in what they call 'blank verse', meaning it's not meant to rhyme apart from the two lines at the end:

If wouldst thou bid to stall, a while, the toil
By which we do make good our rank apparel
Here might thee press, and make witness thereto
Some beacon that brings on a sunrise blush
The while its twin to signal stage attained
Within the task's progress, in manner still

Attend the portent fixed thereon the door
Which oft a proud defiance may bring on
Absent this glow then shall the portal yield
Unto thine touch
Then for the recommencement of the act
At mark the same as was the stay invoked
Affect some pressure to the yielding point
And waters shall once more thy garb anoint

Here's another example. In the popular 2008 film 'Taken', starring Liam Neeson, there's a speech that I expect most of my readers will know or at least have heard of. I'm referring to the 'a very particular set of skills' speech. I can't reproduce it here because it's copyright but you can find it online.

Here's my Fakespeare version. You may like to imagine this in Liam Neeson's voice:

> Thou art unknown to me, thy quest the same.
> Perchance one haul of gold crests thy intent?
> Alas, I'll make report wealth have I none; yet I declare
> Some rarest skills I may perform
> Obtained by thorough toil of seasons past
> By which I'd conjure wraiths unto thy rest
> Thy nights all through then made as horror show
> Save if thou shall relent, unclasp my child
> Relinquished to the bosom of my care, then all is done
> And voids the seed of consequence; seek shall I not
> Due reparation rained on this transgress.
> Yet if ye set a grim course alternate, confound this call
> Then shall I fix thy visage for mine quest
> All certain to obtain thy dark location
> And from thy flesh rip life, 'til all's cessation.

I'm told it's now possible for anyone to create things like this in about five seconds using some sort of AI writing tool.

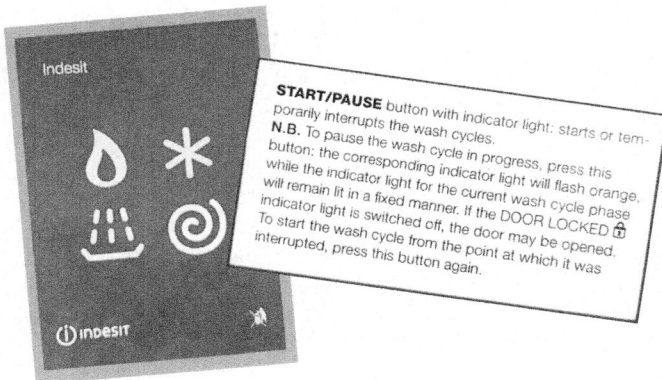

START/PAUSE button with indicator light: starts or temporarily interrupts the wash cycles.
N.B. To pause the wash cycle in progress, press this button: the corresponding indicator light will flash orange, while the indicator light for the current wash cycle phase will remain lit in a fixed manner. If the DOOR LOCKED 🔒 indicator light is switched off, the door may be opened. To start the wash cycle from the point at which it was interrupted, press this button again.

Areas Of Expertise

In this chapter, I mentioned that it's tremendously useful to build up a large network of friends and contacts. Even if you don't actually become 'friends' with someone, it can still be a good idea to keep in touch so you can contact one another if the need arises. The point is that everyone has their skills, aptitudes and experience. You never know when someone else might be able to help you or vice versa.

I know a *lot* of people all over the world. Some are close, valued friends while others are people I only know through social media. Nonetheless, they all have their distinctive areas of 'know how'. When I was preparing this book, just out of curiosity, I went online and asked people I know about their niche areas of expertise. Here's a small selection of the replies I received.

Anything at all to do with horses — including breeding, feeding, riding and training them / Puppetry / The music business from the producer and audio engineer's point of view / Spiders / The music of Grieg / The history of comic books / Fairies in late Victorian and early Edwardian children's literature / Mysticism and secular spirituality.

The history and folklore of vampires / The various designs of Daleks from 1963 to the present day / Carpentry and metalwork / Chemistry and, more specifically, the manufacture of automotive paint / Every episode of 'The Hitchhiker's Guide to the Galaxy' / Competitive curling / Sailing and yachting / The history of the Marx Brothers / the UK tax system.

Indigenous knowledge systems and the memory methods used by oral cultures / The Japanese Kaiju film genre / Lipodema (a medical condition) / The playing style of New Orleans pianist James Booker / The history and repair of wristwatches / Somatic experiencing / Exposed stitch bookbinding.

Insect biology / Sexual dimorphism / Everything there is to know about balloons / Science-fiction, 1850-1925 / Two rare chess openings: the Portsmouth Gambit and the Tayler Opening / protocol analysis at all layers of TCP/IP, AppleTalk, IPX/SPX, Ethernet and Token Ring / The music of Gary Numan / Sailing and yachting / Building plastic scale models / Origami / The history of organised crime / Being a DJ in the days of vinyl records / Krav Maga.

I think you'll agree that's quite a list! The range and scope of the replies I received left me rather astounded. Will I ever *need* any of this expertise? I can't say for sure, although in some cases it does seem rather unlikely. Perhaps I live a remarkably sheltered life, but I can usually make it through the week without knowing *anything* about competitive curling or James Booker. Nonetheless, I *love* the fact that people I know offer such a wealth of knowledge and expertise.

(I confidently expect that as soon as I publish this book, I'll discover an urgent need to know about either competitive curling or James Booker. This is just how life goes.)

Two puppets made by my multi-talented friend Katherine Rhodes

Part Two: Talking

4. Before You Talk

"When we seek for connection, we restore the world to wholeness. Our seemingly separate lives become meaningful as we discover how truly necessary we are to each other."

— Margaret Wheatley

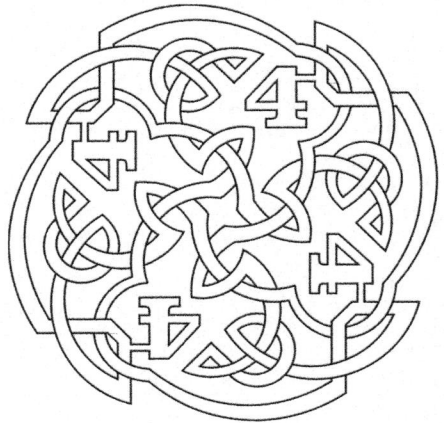

Progress Check

Part One was about the three foundations of People Joy:

- How you feel about other people.

- How you feel about conversations.

- How you feel about yourself.

With these foundations covered, we can now move on to Part Two. This is about ideas and principles that lead to positive, productive and successful conversations. First of all, let's look at ways to *prepare* for good conversations.

May I once again ask you to remind yourself of the *benefits* of People Joy that I mentioned in the Introduction: achieving success, enjoying an easier life, building your professional skills and so on. People Joy is *transformative*. It leads to lasting benefits and can radically improve your life and the lives of those you meet.

Part 1: Foundations

1. About Other People
2. About Yourself
3. About Conversations

Part 2: Talking

4. Before You Talk
5. When You Talk (1)
6. When You Talk (2)
7. When You Talk (3)
8. After You Talk

Part 3: Refinements

9. The Ten-second Smile
10. Voice Magic
11. More About Other People
12. More About You
13. The Joy Of Disagreement
14. Dealing With Anger

Part 4: Special Skills

15. The Art Of Selling
16. The Art Of Persuasion
17. The Art Of Cold Reading
18. Love Is What Works

Prepare Your Shop Window (Part 1)

The first part of preparing to have great, successful conversations is to work on your 'shop window'. Let me explain what I mean by this.

Most shops and stores try to make sure their window sends out the right message and encourages people to step inside. The window usually makes it clear what they sell ('Bridal Dresses') and why you might be interested ('Summer Sale Now On!').

All of your non-verbal communication (NVC) is your metaphorical 'shop window'. I'm referring mainly to your facial expression, especially your eyes, your body language (stance, posture, movement and sense of energy) and sense of personal space. All these aspects of your NVC send out a message to the rest of the world, all the time, everywhere you go. This message affects *how many* conversations you're likely to have and the *quality* of those conversations.

Unfortunately, most people have a shop window that's either neutral or slightly negative, insular and discouraging. It says, 'I am locked inside my own world, with my own thoughts and concerns. I'm wearing a blank expression because it would never occur to me to do anything else. I'm not even thinking of communicating with you or with anyone around me. Basically, my world is me.'

People can go around with this attitude if they want. However, it doesn't encourage good or successful communication. For People Joy purposes, it's a good idea to make sure your shop window works *for* you rather than *against* you. Try to make sure that *every* aspect of your NVC conveys a warm, receptive message that encourages connection and conversation.

A good way to do this is to use a mind script. The next time you're out in public, try running the following words through your mind. As you do, let these words and thoughts affect your facial expression, your body language and your energy. Let the sentiments flow and glow through your body:

> 'My life's in fairly good shape these days. I'm having quite a good day. You don't have to talk to me, of course, but if you did you'd probably enjoy it. I'm approachable, I like people, I have a good sense of humour and I enjoy a good conversation.'

To be emphatically clear, I am not suggesting you say any of this out loud. Simply run these thoughts *through your mind* and let them suffuse your entire presence, including your facial expression. When I do this, I find it produces the mildest trace of a smile on my face, so I look receptive and good-natured. It changes my body language from 'closed off' to 'happy to talk' and lifts my energy a little.

It's easy to exaggerate or parody this idea to make it sound ridiculous. I am *not* suggesting you go through life with a weird grin on your face as if you're desperate for people to like you. All I'm suggesting is that you run the script through your mind as a way to *subtly* transform all of your non-verbal signals. The aim is to convey a positive, receptive spirit, rather than a closed or hostile one, so you look alert and seem willing and happy to communicate.

Your non-verbal signals, your 'shop window', convey a message to people around you all the time. For People Joy purposes, make sure it's a positive one that encourages conversation and connection.

Prepare Your Shop Window (Part 2)

Here are some further aspects of working on your shop window. You'll find it easier to have great and successful conversations if all of the following are true.

You come across as healthy. Anyone meeting you gets the impression you watch what you eat, get enough fruit and veg and make a reasonable effort to lead a healthy life.

You come across as reasonably fit. It looks like you take some exercise once in a while and at least make an effort to look after yourself and stay in reasonably good shape.

You're nice to be near because you keep yourself clean and maintain good personal hygiene. You also smell good because you use a pleasant perfume or aftershave that suits you.

You dress fairly well, your clothes fit and you understand that 'casual' doesn't have to mean scruffy or unclean.

You make an effort when it comes to self-presentation, such as having a decent haircut, clean shoes and clean fingernails.

It's fair to say that most people find it hard to achieve perfection in all of these areas. All I'm suggesting is that the *closer* you can get to this ideal picture, the easier it becomes to have great conversations and reap the benefits. We can't all be handsome or beautiful. We *can* all try to make the most of what we've got.

Why is this beneficial in terms of People Joy? I don't think there's anything mysterious about it. There's a reason why people dress nicely on a first date. When you show you can look after yourself, this subtly suggests you can look after other people as well. It says something about your potential to be a good friend, neighbour, partner, co-worker or business partner. Looking reasonably good, or at least making the best of what you've got, is a subtle way to announce effort and capability. People find this reassuring on an instinctive level.

Incidentally, none of this contradicts what I said in Chapter 1 about *everyone* being worth talking to, even if they don't look too great. The scruffy person who hasn't washed in a while is worth loving, caring about and listening to. They might have a story that would delight and amaze you. With that said, if you want to increase the chances that people will enjoy talking to *you,* getting your shop window in good shape will help a little..

Manners And Mouthwash

To finish off this short 'Before you talk' chapter, here are two final points to consider.

Manners

For People Joy purposes, it's always a good idea to be polite and observe whatever are regarded as 'good manners' in your town, your society and your culture. You may think this sounds like trite advice that 'everyone knows'. However, not everyone follows it.

'Please' and 'thank you' are your free tickets to a lifetime of open doors, warm welcomes and golden opportunities. Conversely, bad manners are free tickets to a lot of closed doors, both real and metaphorical. Making an effort to be polite shows respect for yourself as well as everyone you meet. It's often said that good manners cost nothing. However, bad manners cost a *lot*. They can discourage people from wanting to buy from you, hire you, work for you or ever see you again. I've seen supposedly experienced sales professionals let sales slip through their fingers simply because they failed to be polite and respectful. This never needs to happen. If you want to take a risk, err on the side of being told you're *too* polite.

Good manners can have a relaxing and calming effect in many situations. As Shakespeare puts it so well:

"The mannered way, well tutored charm
Such as presents a courteous style
Can lay on tyrant seas a calm
And even furious storms beguile"
(Measure For Measure, Act III, scene ii.)

Mouthwash Matters

Here's a simple yet effective way to improve every conversation you'll ever have: make sure your breath is fresh and pay attention to your oral hygiene.

When you know you're going to be talking to people, make a point of cleaning your teeth, flossing and using mouthwash. It's easy to do and doesn't take long. You can get small 'travel-size' toothbrushes, tubes of toothpaste and bottles of mouthwash to have with you whenever you feel you might need them. Fresh breath doesn't guarantee a good conversation. Foul breath guarantees a bad one.

It's hard to have a great conversation if, when you talk to someone, they wonder why you've spent all day gargling with onions and fish guts. All of this is especially applicable if you happen to be a smoker. In saying this, I'm not judging you or casting aspersions. I was a smoker myself for a while, many years ago. All I'm saying is that pre-conversational oral hygiene is even more important for you than it is for *everyone* else.

Chapter Summary

This short chapter was about *preparing* to have good, successful conversations. The main headings were:

- Prepare your shop window (part 1). (Mainly about your non-verbal communication.)

- Prepare your shop window (part 2). (About health, diet, fitness etc.)

- Manners and mouthwash.

You've done all the preparation! Now it's time to actually start talking to people... which is the subject of the next chapter.

DUCK

The Perfect Role Model

As the author of this book, I naturally feel the need to be the perfect role model with regard to *everything* I've written about maintaining high standards of self-presentation. For this reason, this is how I look all the time, everywhere I go.

This isn't actually true (surprise!). This picture was taken at a gig in 2005. I was in my penguin suit because I was due to speak and perform at a 'black tie' event. The Lamborghini was being used to transport guests to and from the conference centre. I simply asked if I could stand next to it for a photo.

At the time this photo was taken, the producers of the James Bond films were searching for someone to replace Pierce Brosnan. Inexplicably, they eventually chose Daniel Craig instead of me. Although he turned out to be *quite* good, I think we can all agree the producers made a terrible mistake. Ah well, their loss.

The truth is that I most certainly do *not* claim to be the perfect role model in all of the areas mentioned in this chapter. Far from it! I am a rich abundance of flaws and imperfections. My appearance bears witness to the tragedy of human weakness and poor self-discipline. I'm sometimes overweight and I have never, in my life, been regarded as 'well dressed'.

In any collection
Of mortal perfection
You'll see that they missed
My name off the list

However, despite my numerous conspicuous flaws and personal failings, when I'm out in public I make a reasonable effort to appear socially acceptable and not *entirely* repulsive. When I walk down the street, mothers don't instinctively gather their children up safely in their arms, tracking me with a baleful 'Mama Tiger' stare, while dogs back away whimpering. Well, at least not *every* time.

In any case, the merits of the ideas in this book are independent of my personal ability to implement them. 'Don't stick your head in a wasp's nest' would still be good advice even if I personally did it three times a week.

5. When You Talk: Seven Keys

"What do we live for, if it is not to make life less difficult for each other?"

— *George Eliot*

Progress Check

In Part One, we looked at the three foundations of People Joy.

Now, in Part Two, we're looking at conversational techniques. The previous chapter presented some good ideas you can use *before* you actually say anything. In this chapter, I'll present seven good ideas to keep in mind once you actually start talking.

Your Starting Point

Let me summarise the ideas we've looked at so far.

You appreciate that people are endlessly, beautifully fascinating. They often have 'hidden depths'. They are all worth talking to and listening to. The more different they are from yourself, the more fascinating they are.

You practise self-greatness and are free from self-doubt, fear and conflict (or at least trying to be). Before you talk, you think to yourself, 'It's great to be me and I expect it's great to be you too.'

You see every conversation as a chance to win. You don't talk to people with a blank expression, eyes that don't say anything, a flat voice and low personal energy. You let the person you're going to talk to *see* and *feel* the genuine warmth of your interest in who they are and their story.

You've taken care of your 'shop window' so you look good-natured, pleasant and alert to the *possibility* of having a good conversation. Your body language is open and receptive. Even if you're not one of life's beautiful people, you've made a reasonable effort to look presentable and your breath is fresh.

Instead of having conversations that are passive and lack intention, you choose to have ones that are active and intentional. For this reason, you are mentally alert and switched-on, rather than relying on conversational autopilot. You appreciate that every conversation is a chance to enjoy a win. This usually takes one of three forms:

- To go on a mind walk.

- To achieve something positive.

- To build a good connection.

This is your People Joy starting point. Good! You are all set to enjoy the art, magic and power of successful conversations.

1. The Att Chat Principle

First **attention,** *then* **chat.**

Always make sure you have someone's *attention* before you try to have a meaningful *conversation*. I know this sounds like advice from Planet Obvious but it's surprising how often people *don't* do this.

Imagine a fairly busy office. Andy wants to ask Carol what time the sales meeting starts. He faces towards Carol's desk, raises his voice and hurls his question in her direction. As there's quite a bit of background noise, Carol remains unaware that Andy is asking a question and remains focused on her work. Andy raises his voice a little more and tries again. Carol is now vaguely aware that Andy is asking her something, or at least grunting in a semi-coherent manner, but it will take her a few seconds to save her work and switch her attention to him.

Andy, having now asked his question twice, starts feeling exasperated. Carol, meanwhile, doesn't *even* know what the question is.

"When *is* it?" asks Andy, impatiently.

"When's what?" replies Carol, suitably puzzled.

"The *meeting!*"

"What meeting?"

Andy has to start all over again, clarifying the nature of his question.

Back in the days when I had a regular office job, I saw people make this mistake all the time. On countless occasions, I saw one person try to talk to another or ask a question *without* first of all getting their attention. This is absurd, like expecting someone to catch a ball when they don't *even* know you've thrown it to them. The same thing happens *every* day in thousands of offices, shops, factories, schools and homes. Each single instance may not *seem* to be much of a problem. However, they add up to a vast amount of wasted time, frayed tempers and mis-communication.

This never needs to happen. *First* make sure you have the other person's attention. *Then* start the conversation.

The Double Start

Here's a subtle refinement to the Att Chat Principle. When you have gained someone's attention, use a double start like this:

"I want to ask you... I want to ask you what time this afternoon's team meeting is due to start?"

Or, in a different context, you might say something like:

"Can you please hand me... can you please hand me the rota for this week's warehouse shifts?"

I know this looks distinctly odd on the printed page. However, in a real-life conversation it doesn't have to sound odd at all. The point is that quite often, when it *looks* as if you've got someone's attention, their mind is still lagging a second or two behind. Even if they have turned to face you, so you have eye contact, it might still be a second or two before you have their *mental* attention. The double start helps the other person to lock on to you, so to speak, and be receptive to whatever you want to say.

2. Start Smart

You, This Or Me?

In some cases, you don't get to choose how a conversation starts. This will be determined by the other person or by the context. When you *do* get to choose, you have three basic options:

- Say something about the other person (that they will enjoy hearing).

- Say something about the current situation or context in which you both find yourselves.

- Say something about yourself.

Option (1) is usually the best one to take. Option (2) is often almost as good, depending on the circumstances. Option (3) is least likely to be successful in People Joy terms. Use it reluctantly if you have to use it at all.

When you take option (1), you immediately convey something important to the other person: you intend to have an *outward-facing* conversation rather than endlessly talking about yourself. You are reassuring them that they aren't going to get trapped in your personal fishbowl of stagnant self-absorption.

Option (1) involves say something about the other person *that they will enjoy hearing*. It's hard to give specific examples because obviously a lot depends on the context, your personality and your conversational style. The best I can do is to repeat a point I made in Chapter 3. Rather than wondering *what* to say, focus instead on your *intention*. Let your intention be your guide and the words will follow fairly easily. Remember, your intention in People Joy terms is to achieve a *win:* enjoy a mind walk, achieve something positive or build a connection. If you keep this in mind, it shouldn't be hard to say something the OP will enjoy hearing.

Suppose you're striking up a conversation with a stranger. Perhaps you could express a bit of friendly sympathy with the fact that they have a lot to carry, or they're dealing with two toddlers, or the queue is moving really slowly. Another option is to mention something you have in common. Maybe their T-shirt suggests you like the same music or they're carrying a book by an author you like.

If you've been introduced to someone at a social event, please don't say, "I've heard a lot about you". First of all, it's a cliché which suggests you've drifted back into autopilot mode. Secondly, it's unhelpfully ambiguous, since the things you've heard could be really *bad* things or simply inaccurate! It's better to be specific and positive. For example: "It's good to meet you! Jane's been telling me about all the great work you do at the school."

Let's return to our three 'Start Smart' choices. Option (2) works almost as well as the first option and is sometimes more appropriate. The basic idea is to say something *relatable* and *inclusive* about the situation that you and the OP both happen to be in. For example, let's suppose you're in the staff canteen: "There's been a miracle... the microwave's actually working! Hard to believe. That's two days in row. A new record!"

Option (3) is to say something about yourself. The *only* time to start a conversation this way is when it's what the other person *wants* and *expects*, and when it would seem strange *not* to.

3. Signs Of Sameness

Play the game of 'we're the same'.

When people talk to one another, any perceived similarity feels good and reassuring. It suggests, 'We'll find it easy to get along'. Lack of similarity feels awkward and challenging. It suggests, 'We're going to struggle to achieve understanding'. This being the case, always try to give whoever you're talking to the sense that you are similar people, at least in *some* ways, and that you have a few things in common.

All the techniques in this section call for subtlety and nuance. If the other person *notices* you using them, they will distract from the conversation rather than enhancing it. Like a marionette's strings, they work best when noticed least.

Silent Signs Of Sameness

Let's start with *non-verbal* ways to convey sameness and similarity. One subtle technique is to match the *breathing* and *energy level* of the other person. Aim to breathe in and out *approximately* as often as the OP and to match their personal energy, whether it be high or low. This is an extremely subtle way to create a feeling of similarity.

Another popular technique is called 'mirroring'. This features in many guides to inter-personal skills. The general idea is that you subtly copy *some* aspects of the OP's behaviour, almost as if you were their mirror image. For example, you might mirror their general stance, the inclination of their head, how their hold their hands, some of their gestures and so on. To repeat for emphasis, subtlety matters. If the OP detects — even for a second — that you're playing a strange game of 'copy cat', this will feel distinctly uncomfortable. It helps to remember that you don't always have to mirror a particular gesture or behaviour *immediately*. For example, if you aim to match the other person's stance, you can do so gradually, little by little, during the conversation. It doesn't have to happen straight away.

Another good signal of sameness is to modify your position with regard to the OP. Instead of standing or sitting face to face, aim to reach the point where you and the OP are in a 'ten minutes to two' position (as on a traditional clock face). Convert the 'me against you' feeling to one that says 'you and I are on the same side'.

Verbal Signs Of Sameness

Let's move on to verbal signs of sameness. The first technique is to talk at roughly the same *pace* as the other person. You don't need to aim for total accuracy or get out a stopwatch. Just aim to *broadly* match the OP's vocal pace, rhythm and cadences so you don't *seem* noticeably slower or faster.

Another good technique is to use some of the same colloquial expressions as the OP. Suppose that the OP, referring to something being unlikely to happen, uses the expression, "never in a month of Sundays". Later on, look for a chance to use the same expression. You could say, "...and I just knew it wasn't going to happen. Like you said earlier, I got that 'never in a month of Sundays' feeling." (By definition, colloquial expressions vary from one country and culture to another. Feel free to substitute any expression you like in the example I've just given.)

When you start a conversation, look for opportunities to highlight anything that you and the OP have in common. Four good ways to do this involve referring to:

- Likes and dislikes. You both like (or dislike) the same TV shows, movies, music, fashion, sports or food.

- Employment. You used to work in the trade or industry they mentioned, or you know someone who does, or it's a job that's always intrigued you and you have a few questions.

- Geography. You have lived or worked in a place the OP mentioned, or you've been there, or you've heard about it or it's a place you'd like to visit one day.

- Story. You and the OP have something in common in terms of your story, background or past experience.

You can remember these four options using the mnemonic 'LEGS'. It's a good idea to look for one of these points of relatable connection early on in *every* conversation. The longer you've been alive, the easier this is to do. Older people have seen, done and experienced more things than younger people and therefore have a longer list of things they can relate to. This is one of the very, very few advantages of getting older.

4. Read The Room

Be sufficiently shrewd to notice the mood.

'Reading the room' means being *aware* of what's happening during a conversation, in terms of mood and feelings, and *responding* in a constructive way.

This is something that all performers and entertainers do during *every* show. We are constantly scanning the audience, second by second, to gauge how well things are going. Do I need to take the pace up or down a little? Is one part of the audience not feeling involved — and how can I fix this? Good performers are constantly reading the room in this way and making adjustments to deliver the best show they can. It takes hundreds of hours of what we call 'flying time' (practical performing experience) to refine this sensitivity.

At the start of a conversation, do your best to assess the emotional state of the other person. In many cases, the OP may be in a fairly normal mood and having a fairly normal day. The point is to give yourself the *opportunity* to notice anything unusual. Is the OP happy and relaxed or stressed and tired? Do they seem comfortable or anxious? If you had to guess, would you say they've had a great day so far or a tiring and frustrating one?

If there's anything negative about the OP's emotional state, can you help them shift to a better state? If they seem nervous, can you help them to feel more relaxed and confident? If they're a bit dejected, can you be a good listener and help them to feel more positive?

Also, take a second to consider what the OP *wants* from the conversation in emotional terms. For example, perhaps they are yearning for a bit of praise and validation that they should be getting from elsewhere but aren't. Perhaps, in a workplace situation, they are struggling to cope but don't feel they can say so. Sometimes, people have a lot on their mind and want to be heard and understood.

Here's another point to consider: is the other person happy with the environment? For example, if the OP is mildly autistic, a busy, noisy atmosphere might cause them to feel over-stimulated. If the OP has asthma, they might be feeling uncomfortable because of the humidity or dust in the air. If the environment is a problem, see if you can move somewhere more conducive to a relaxed, enjoyable conversation.

It's not hard to develop some emotional empathy. In any case, trying is always more successful than *not* trying. As the conversation progresses, *remain* sensitive to the other person's mood and feelings. Continue to 'read the room', so to speak, and make whatever subtle changes will help you achieve the best conversation you can have.

Group Dynamics

You can apply 'read the room' sensitivity to group conversations. For example, take care of whatever introductions may be necessary. If there's someone in the group you don't know, introduce yourself and help them to see how you 'fit in' with the group:

> "Hi, I don't think we've met. My name's Ian. I'm here with Maria. We've been friends ever since we worked at the same company twenty years ago."

If you can perform useful introductions for other people in the group, do so. Always take the opportunity to introduce people in a way that's kind and flattering:

> "Does everyone know each other? Alice, I don't think you've met my amazing friend Michael yet. He was one of the founders of 'Monday Night Magic' and is a highly successful agent."

Reading the room in a group setting also involves being *situationally* aware. Take a moment to check if anyone feels excluded from the conversation. Sometimes, just making a minor adjustment to the way people are standing or sitting can make someone feel more included in the circle. Nobody likes to feel left out. Also, see if anyone feels they are being talked over and, if so, fix the problem. For example, in group situations it's regrettably common for men to talk over women. Try to prevent this from happening:

> "Thanks for that summary, Jeff. I'd love to hear Linda's take on this. [To Linda] You've handled situations like this before, haven't you? What would you suggest?"

Learning to read the room delivers countless benefits for you and the people you talk to. The more sensitive you are to how people are feeling, the more successful you'll be (whether you're performing or having a conversation). Sensitivity always makes sense.

A Conversation Is Never Just A Conversation

Here's one final part of 'reading the room'. In her excellent book, 'That's Not What I Meant', Deborah Tannen makes the point that a conversation is never *just* a conversation. She suggests you should always pay attention to the *emotional subtext* of the conversation.

Tannen gives the example of a couple having an argument. She explains that one partner might be thinking about the *facts* of the matter and who is right or wrong. The other partner might be thinking about these things as well but *also* wondering, 'What does this say about the state of our relationship?'

Pay attention to the conversation itself but also try to remain aware of the bigger picture. What's the subtext? What's the other person's emotional state? Develop the habit of reminding yourself that 'a conversation is never just a conversation'. I think you'll find this makes a significant difference to the conversations you have.

5. The Name Game

CUR: Check, Use and Remember their name.

In his justly famous book, 'How To Win Friends And Influence People', Dale Carnegie wrote that a person's name is, to them, the most musical sound in the world. It was a good point when Carnegie wrote the book (1936) and it's still a good point today.

When you are introduced to someone, *check* that you get their name right. If you need them to clarify their name, for example if it's unfamiliar to you or from a different culture, politely ask them to help you say their name correctly. There are three good reasons to do this. One, it means you don't inadvertently give offence later on by getting their name wrong. Two, it facilitates a good connection. Three, you'll learn about the incredible richness and diversity of names from around the world. (See this chapter's DUCK for examples.)

Next, try to *use* the OP's name during the conversation. It's a nice thing to do and helps to cement their name in your memory. If you want to, you can study mnemonics and learn a few ways to remember people's names. This usually involves creating a mental association between their name and their appearance.

Another good idea is to use the OP's name at the *end* of the conversation, when you say goodbye. Take one last mental snapshot of who you've been talking to and mentally say their name to yourself. These days, in many social or business situations, you're likely to come away with some record of the person's name such as their business card or social media details. If you don't, make a *written* note of their name as soon as you can. Write it down instead of trusting yourself to remember. A pencil *never* forgets.

While I'm on the subject of writing things down, one simple way to improve your conversations is to make notes when people mention things of interest. Let the OP know what you're doing: "I'm not ignoring you. I'm making a note because that sounds like a book I'd enjoy reading." Making notes — and being *seen* to make them — is a good move in People Joy terms. It signals to the OP that you're actually *listening*, you *care* about what they're saying and you *appreciate* the things that they're telling you.

6. Match The Mode

Facts, feelings or fun?

In most conversations, the person you're talking to wants to focus on facts, feelings or, if they're in a light-hearted mood, just having fun. Always strive to be sensitive to this distinction. These three modes of conversation may overlap at times but they are not identical. You will be doing both yourself and the OP a favour if you try to 'tune in' to whichever mode they are using: facts, feelings, fun.

If one person is primarily focused on facts and figures while the other is talking about feelings and emotions, they are unlikely to enjoy a successful conversation. This distinction isn't important in *every* conversation, of course. Just be aware that it does *sometimes* matter and that getting the mode wrong can lead to annoyance and hurt feelings. If you aren't using the same conversational mode at first, one of you is going to have to change modes and it's probably you.

The distinction between facts and feelings isn't always clear cut. People sometimes discuss facts in quite an emotional way or vice versa. However, if you at least *try* to make sure that you and the other person are using the same conversational mode, you will reduce friction and enjoy far more productive conversations.

7. Chat Ratios

Balance the talking and the listening.

During *every* conversation, try to remain aware of how much time you spend *talking* versus how much time you spend *listening*. I call this the 'chat ratio'.

Poor chat ratio sensitivity is one of the commonest ways in which people inadvertently sabotage their conversations. The chance to have what *could* have been a happy, brilliant and productive chat gets wasted because someone either spoke too much or not enough.

In lieu of any good reason to do otherwise, aim for an approximate 50:50 balance. Of course, this is subject to context. If someone is asking you questions because they want to learn from you, it's appropriate for you to do most of the talking while they do most of the listening. Conversely, if someone has been through a difficult time and wants to talk about it, you should do your best to be a good listener. The chat ratio is also subject to other factors, such as how socially confident you feel and how easy you find it to express yourself. The basic point is to be *aware* of the chat ratio. Try to avoid giving the other person the feeling that you are talking either too much or too little.

I know there's a piece of traditional wisdom that goes like this: 'You've got two ears and one mouth for a reason. Listen twice as much as you talk'. No one *ever* seems to mention the obvious problem: what if *both* people are trying to follow this advice?

There's one refinement I'd like to add. Don't make the common mistake of thinking that just because it's your *turn* to talk you have to talk *about yourself*. Your turn doesn't have to be *about* you. You could use your turn to talk about the OP, comment on what they said, mention a third party, ask another question and so on. 'My turn' doesn't have to mean 'more about me'.

There may be situations where *you* are sensitive to the chat ratio but the OP isn't. You may end up (a) doing all the listening while they tediously recite their entire life story, or (b) carrying the conversation while the OP is more or less mute. This might not feel especially good from your point of view. However, at least *you* are not the one causing the OP to feel that the conversation isn't all that satisfying.

Painless Practice

In this chapter, I've presented seven good ideas you can use when you talk to people. Let me add a brief note about how to *practice* using these ideas. There's a notion in the magic world that I'm sure is found in all sorts of other areas as well. It's this: 'Practise when it *doesn't* matter so you'll be good when it *does*.' Here's an example. Suppose a magician is learning a card trick where, just by estimation, she needs to cut a deck of cards exactly in half at will. She can practise by regularly performing a *different* card trick that involves cutting the deck but where it doesn't matter if she gets exactly half or not. Every time she performs this other trick, she *aims* for half just for the practice, knowing she can fail without pain. She practises the move when it *doesn't* matter so she'll be good when it *does*.

You can apply the same thinking to all the ideas in this book. You will have many different conversations in your life, some more important than others. You can practise your People Joy skills during relatively *unimportant* conversations as preparation for when the *important* ones come along. Every chat is a chance for some painless practice.

Chapter Summary

In this chapter, I shared seven good ideas that will help you to have better, more successful conversations:

- The att chat principle.

- Start smart.

- Signs of sameness.

- Read the room.

- The name game.

- . Match the mode.

- Chat ratios.

The next chapter contains seven *more* good ideas to go with them!

DUCK

Names Unlimited

In this chapter I mentioned the amazing range of first names to be found all over the world. It seems that almost any combination of sounds or letters is a first name *somewhere*. While working on this chapter, I asked my friends about common first names in their country that someone who only speaks English, like me, might struggle to say or write correctly. Here are some of the replies I received:

Belgium: Ine (pronounced so it rhymes with 'keener').
Finland: Yrjö, Niilo.
India: Pratiksha, Hrithik, Aishwarya, Aayushmaan.
Indonesia: Nyoman, Ketut, Made (Made is pronounced Mah-day, said quickly).

Ireland: Maedbh, Eoghan, Aoife, Niamh, Caoimhe.
Israel: Moshé, Yehonatan.
Lithuania: Beatrice (pronounced Bee-ah-tritch-eh).
Netherlands: Noud.

Nigeria: Ngozichukwuka.
Norway: Anbjørg, Setesdal.
Poland: Woitek.
Sweden: Torbjörn, Asbjörn.

Turkey: Oğuz, Abdurrahman, Süyümbike.
Wales: Myfanwy, Lleucu, Myfyr.

I find it rather amazing that all of these combinations of letters and sounds are a common first name *somewhere* in the world. I don't currently have any friends called Ngozichukwuka but I hope I will one day. I think it's an awesome name!

Also, this list merely confirms something that many English people, including myself, have suspected for a long time: Irish names are a prank they play on the rest of the world. 'Hey, let's put together *any* combination of letters we want, pretend it's a name and watch English people try *and fail* to pronounce it.'

(It was fun running my spell-checker on this page.)

A Sales Line That Doesn't Work

In this chapter, I mentioned the value of 'signs of sameness'. In the retail sphere, I've noticed some sales people try to use this idea in a way that doesn't work and is counterproductive. It goes like this. Imagine a store full of different makes and models of washing machines. A customer browses for a while and then indicates a preference for Model X. The sales person immediately smiles and says, "Good choice! That's the one I've got at home, actually." In other words, whatever the customer chooses, the sales person claims that they use it or have bought it themselves, as if this bestows a magical glow of excellence on the item.

Please don't ever use this line. Everyone can see through it. The customer knows perfectly well that the sales person would have said exactly the same thing if they had pointed to any other product in the store. This being the case, the sales person has just killed off their credibility and any sense of trust they might otherwise have been able to build with the customer.

There *are* good ways to use signs of sameness in selling and in any environment where you'd like to practise People Joy. However, the 'That's the one I use!' line isn't one of them.

6. When You Talk: Seven More Keys

"The most important thing in communication is hearing what isn't said."

— *Peter Drucker*

Progress Check

Part Two of People Joy consists of good ideas you can use *before* you talk to people, *when* you talk to them and *after* you talk to them.

We've looked at seven good ideas to bear in mind when you talk to people (from 'Att Chat' to 'Chat Ratios'). In this chapter, I'm going to share seven more.

Part 1: Foundations	Part 2: Talking
1. About Other People 2. About Yourself 3. About Conversations	4. Before You Talk 5. When You Talk (1) 6. When You Talk (2) 7. When You Talk (3) 8. After You Talk
Part 3: Refinements	Part 4: Special Skills
9. The Ten-second Smile 10. Voice Magic 11. More About Other People 12. More About You 13. The Joy Of Disagreement 14. Dealing With Anger	15. The Art Of Selling 16. The Art Of Persuasion 17. The Art Of Cold Reading 18. Love Is What Works

1. The Golf Principle

Don't care about golf? Care about the golfer!

This is a hugely important principle if you want to enjoy better and more productive conversations. I sincerely believe this can transform your life.

Let's say you've met someone who is talking about how much they love playing golf. If you also play golf, this will naturally lead to quite a lively conversation. However, if you don't play golf, you might be inclined to adopt a 'switched off' face and look bored. "Golf, huh? Mm. I don't play." In some cases, you might also feel inclined to say something rather dismissive, as if 'This subject doesn't interest *me*' is the same as 'This subject isn't interesting'. I often see people react in this way and I think it's a terrible waste of an opportunity.

In this type of situation, take an interest in the *person* rather than the *subject*. Relish the opportunity to go on a mind walk. Be honest about the fact that either (a) you don't know much about the subject or (b) it's not something that has *ever* interested you. However, you can still take an interest in the *person* you're talking to and *why* this subject means a lot to them. You can say things like:

> "You know, I've never really understood the appeal of golf so I'm fascinated. Tell me how you got into it and why you think you took to it so readily."

> "Why do you think you love it so much? What do you get out of it? For you, what's the essence of its appeal? Are there things about the game that you *don't* like?"

I am not suggesting you fire questions at the OP so they feel interrogated. The points is that there are several conversational avenues to explore. Once you're enjoying a conversation like this, you can slip naturally into the role of the curious, intrigued outsider. For example, you can ask a question that the OP, in their role as the expert, will enjoy answering. It's not hard to think of things to ask.

> "I sometimes see golf on TV and there's one bit I don't understand. I might see a golfer sink a really long putt, like thirty feet or so. Then on the next hole, he only needs a short putt of one or two feet and he misses. How can that happen?"

There's *always* something to talk about. If you're talking about a sport, hobby or interest that's really popular, ask the OP why they think it's so popular. Alternatively, if it's something with quite limited appeal, ask them why they think so few people like it.

I've had excellent conversations with people all over the world about subjects I know *nothing* about. Given the truly vast and impressive extent of my ignorance, this covers a *lot* of subjects.

Discover Don't Judge

I need to add one small addition to the above: discover, don't judge. By all means go on a mind walk and explore why the OP feels so passionately about John Coltrane, keeping tropical fish or Danish architecture. Discover all you like but resist the temptation to *judge*. More specifically, don't judge *negatively*. If you want to offer praise, respect or admiration, go right ahead. But if you have something negative to say about whatever the subject is, keep it to yourself.

The Love Hate Question

Let's suppose you're talking to someone who does a job you know nothing about. Here's a wonderful question you can ask:

> "I don't know anything about [the job you do]. However, there are a few things about it that I, as a complete outsider, could probably guess. But just out of interest, let me ask you this. Tell me one thing you really love about the work, and one thing you hate (or at least dislike) that I, as a complete outsider, would probably never guess. Things I'd find surprising."

I've asked many people this question over the years. It always leads to delightful, fascinating answers that you'd never guess in a hundred years! You can ask the same question about someone's hobby, pastime or area of interest that you know nothing about. Ask about the details that outsiders would find surprising.

2. Find The Glory Of The Story

Find the why behind the what.

On many occasions, I've heard conversations reach a dead end very quickly, like this:

"I'm not available on Tuesdays. That's when I go to my yoga."

"Okay. I'll bear that in mind."

"Have you ever done any yoga or stuff like that?"

"No."

And that's where the conversation ends.

This is a sadly wasted opportunity. Whenever someone mentions what they like or dislike, or anything about their tastes, preferences and opinions, there's a *story* waiting to be discovered. They weren't *born* with a love of yoga or a dislike of jazz. There's always a story behind the opinion they've arrived at. Take an interest in this story and ask them about it.

When people mention something they like or enjoy, ask them how they got into it, why they find it interesting and why it's important to them. When they mention things they dislike, delve a little deeper. What, specifically, has led them to dislike it or not enjoy it? How come all the things that other people like about it (whatever it is) hasn't had any effect on them?

This technique helps you to avoid having shallow conversations and leads to deeper connections with the people you meet. It also makes the other person feel valued and interesting.

This approach often leads to conversations that people haven't had before. Let's say you meet someone who *loves* singing in a choir. It may be the case that all her friends have known about this for years but none have ever asked her *why* she loves the choir so much. In Chapter 3, I talked about seeing every conversation as a chance to achieve a win. If you talk to someone and they say, "You know, no one's ever asked me that before!", you can most definitely count this as a significant win. Well done!

3. Flash The Flags

Show you're aware *before* they despair.

In People Joy terms, a 'flag' is a brief comment that shows you are sensitive to how the other person might be feeling about the conversation. More specifically, it's a comment that *anticipates* possible problems and tries to *defuse* them. Here are a few examples of what flags sound like:

> "I know this story is going on a bit but I guarantee it's worth it and you'll love the way it ends. And then I'll shut up, I promise."

> "I know I'm not saying much but it's not because I'm bored. At the moment I think it's best if I listen and learn. I'll join in a bit more later on."

> "I promise this is relevant to what we're talking about. Let me get to the end and you'll see how it all ties together. Then it's over to you."

Using flags in this way shows the other person that you're considerate, aware of the fact that you're talking quite a lot (or not very much) and that you don't want this to be a problem. You're also promising to be fair and, a little later on, make time for the other person to either talk more or listen more as the case may be.

Verbal flags of this type are a remarkably effective way to improve your conversations. It's a great shame that hardly anyone uses them. I suggest you make a habit of using flags at every appropriate opportunity. They are a wonderful way to convey your awareness of how the conversation is going and your thoughtfulness. Flags can also feel tremendously reassuring. They let the OP know that you aren't going to talk forever, about things that seem irrelevant, while they slowly lose the will to live.

You can't have a great conversation if the other person feels bored (because they feel as if you'll never stop talking). Similarly, it won't be a great conversation if the OP feels bewildered (because they don't see the relevance of what you're talking about) or annoyed (because they feel like they'll never get their turn). Flags are an excellent way to avoid these feelings arising.

4. De-stress Not Distress

Give the relief that calms the grief.

Here's a conversational super power for you to enjoy!

Suppose you ask your colleague, John, to get back to you with some important information. He fails to do so. Later, he gets in touch and is clearly feeling rather guilty about having let you down. You could relish this golden opportunity to vent your rage and displeasure on John, since he is clearly at fault. You could make him squirm while you angrily denounce his pathetic unreliability. You could also give yourself an ego stroke by contrasting your own impressively high reputation for dependability with John's glaring inadequacy.

Alternatively, you could say, " Hey... it's all right. There's no need to apologise. These things happen and you were probably busy with other stuff. Don't worry about it. In the end I was able to get the information from Rachel. It's all right."

Consider another example. Your friend Mary is on her way to meet you but realises she's behind schedule. Maybe she should have set off earlier or she's had travel problems. She calls you, clearly feeling rather bad about the situation, and apologetically lets you know that she's going to be late.

As with the example above, you could seize this excellent chance to tell Mary how pathetically unreliable she is. You might also offer a rather laboured sigh of weary exasperation as you say there's not much you can do except wait until she can be bothered to turn up. You could make it clear how disappointed you are by Mary's deplorable inability to match your own glittering track record of rock-solid punctuality.

Alternatively, you could say, "Oh, please don't worry about it! I know how easy it is to get a bit behind schedule. Listen, just get here when you can and in the meantime, relax and travel safely. I'm really looking forward to seeing you!"

The world is full of things that *add* to how much stress people feel. If you want to practise People Joy, be the person who calms people down, *reduces* their stress and reassures them that there's no need to feel bad. When you help people to go on the journey from distress to de-stress, you're performing a valuable service. You're also taking stress and anxiety out of your *own* spirit and your *own* life. You're helping other people and doing yourself a favour at the same time.

Throughout your life, there will be times when people let you down and fail to be impressively perfect. You'll always have the option of feeling exasperated and loftily superior. I suggest you choose not to do this. Instead, take the much better path: de-stress, not distress. If you want to know why, take a look around you. Do you think the world needs *more* friction, stress and bad feelings? Or a lot less? Do you think it needs *more* people sounding lofty and superior while scolding others and trying to make them feel bad? Or less?

I vote for less. (I'll revisit this subject in Chapter 11.)

5. Positive Reframing

Soothe the shame with a better frame.

'Reframing' means the facts stay the same but you change how you *describe* or *characterise* them. The important part is that reframing can change how people feel about events and experiences. I love positive reframing. It's a highly effective way to brighten someone's day. I also think of it as a type of 'conversational magic trick' because it transforms someone's feelings or reactions from negative to positive (or at least a lot less negative).

Let's imagine a co-worker has just come out of a meeting. She's been told something nasty, such as, "That was without doubt the worst project plan I've ever seen! It was utterly hopeless!"

You can be the good listener who offers a positive reframe:

> "Well, that sounds to me like [Manager] just blowing off steam like he often does. Don't worry — it's just his way. We've all had a roasting off him at one time or another! Look, it was always going to be difficult. You had hardly any time to prepare and you weren't properly briefed. For what it's worth — and I'm being straight with you — I felt that you did a pretty good job under difficult circumstances. Perhaps it wasn't perfect but, trust me, I've seen far worse. Let's sneak off for an early lunch and talk about something else."

Providing people with a touch of positive reframing is a truly loving and beautiful thing to do. Everyone loves a positive re-framer!

You can do the same for yourself. Let's imagine you have a relatively junior role in a company. You get something wrong and an angry warthog of a manager offers an unpleasant comment: "You really messed that up! That was a complete disaster!"

Simply accepting this verdict will cause you to feel bad about yourself, which isn't good for your self-greatness. Alternatively, you can *reframe* it. You can say to yourself:

> "Well, 'messed it up' is a bit harsh. It's true that I didn't perform at my best, but then again no one's perfect. Some parts of [the task] actually turned out pretty well. However, I know I made mistakes. I'm glad I tried, I know I did my best and this is a learning opportunity for me. I'll do better next time."

You don't need to actually *say* all this to anyone but you can *think* it. Internal positive reframing can be soothing for your nerves and good for maintaining healthy self-greatness.

PACE people (Performers, Artists, Creatives, Entertainers) support one another with positive reframing all the time. Given what we do, we all have to deal with unkind and unfair criticism from time to time. Offering one another a bit of positive reframing is part of our mutual support mechanism. It might sound like this:

> "The owner of the club, Ted, said I was the worst act he'd ever seen and I'm third-rate at best and he'll never book me again!"

> "Well, look, we both know it wasn't your finest night or your best performance. I think nerves probably got to you. But listen, I thought you did pretty well overall. You just weren't on your best form, that's all. Anyone can have a bad gig! As for Ted, well, everyone knows his opinions change with the wind. He'll say you're terrible one day and then next time he'll say you're the greatest. You'll show him! Remember, Decca [British record label] turned down the Beatles!"

Whenever you talk to people, look out for opportunities to offer a touch of positive reframing. It costs you nothing but can mean diamonds and sunlight to the person you're talking to.

6. The Handover Principle

Invite them to play with a 'Wouldn't you say?'.

Let's say you're having a conversation and you've been sharing a story or explaining your opinion. When you get to the end, find a way to hand the conversation back to the other person. You can do this using various phrases:

> "...and in the end we were able to get it to work. Have you ever had a problem like that?"

> "...and I think that's a fairer way to do it. Wouldn't you say?"

> "...so I've suggested we get together and discuss it next week. What's your take on it?"

These handover phrases show that you want to enjoy a *conversation* rather than indulge in a *monologue*. They tend to make the other person feel good, whether they realise it or not, because you are clearly expressing your interest in what *they* think or what *they* have to say. When you use a handover phrase like the ones I've suggested, you show that you *want* the conversation to flow easily back and forth, with both parties taking it in turns to make their contribution.

7. I Believe In You

Never be shy to say IBIY.

There are several ways in which you could make the world a better place. For example, you could eradicate disease, give everyone a holiday in Hawaii or perform heroic feats that get written about in history books. However, there's a much simpler way: look for opportunities to tell someone, "I believe in you". Even if you don't use those exact words, you can convey the same general sentiment.

The only rule is that you have to say this *sincerely*. It may help to remember that you can trim your expression of confidence to the point where it sounds credible. Saying 'I believe in you' doesn't have to mean 'you are without doubt going to be greatest success story the world has ever known'. It could just mean you think they've got what it takes to set up their own business.

People often like to talk about their plans, hopes, dreams, ambitions and so on. You may or may not be in a good position to offer welcome and useful *advice*. But you can always express your positive *belief*. One way to do this is to say, "I expect you'll do well." A better way is to add a bit of observation or reasoning, so it sounds like this:

"I expect you'll do well because you tend to plan these things quite thoroughly. Also, you've got some good experience behind you now plus plenty of contacts you can call on for a bit of help if you need it."

You see the difference? The 'because' part means you sound less bland and superficial and more factual and supportive. Always find one or two reasons that support your expression of positive belief. It will mean a lot to the OP.

Talking with someone about their career plans? Let them know you believe in them and expect that, whichever direction they chose to go in, you think they're likely to do well.

Having a chat with someone who's about to be a parent for the first time? Tell them you think they'll be a good parent and will cope well with their new responsibilities.

Talking to a friend who's about to start a new chapter in their life? It's kind and helpful to casually mention that you feel they'll do well and make a success of it.

Provided you can do it sincerely, letting someone know you believe in them is a wonderful thing to do. Many successful people say they owe a lot to someone who, at an early stage in their career, said 'I believe in you' or words to that effect. A simple expression of confidence can make a huge difference to someone's career and determination to pursue their dreams..

When you put this idea into practice, you'll discover something interesting: it doesn't only help the person you're talking to. It makes *you* feel good as well! There's always something satisfying about giving other people a bit of sincere support and encouragement. As the Chinese proverb says, 'A bit of fragrance always clings to the hand that gives the rose.' Who knows what role you might play in someone's success story? (In the DUCK you'll find a story about someone who expressed their belief in *me*, many years ago.)

Chapter Summary

This chapter was about seven more good conversational ideas (to add to the seven in the preceding chapter). They were:

- The golf principle.

- Find the glory of the story.

- Flash the flags.

- De-stress not distress.

- Positive reframing.

- The handover principle.

- I believe in you.

In the next chapter, I'll talk about seven common conversational *mistakes* you need to know about so you can avoid them.

DUCK

A Note Of Gratitude

In this chapter, I referred to the power of saying 'I believe in you'.

This seems an appropriate opportunity to place my own gratitude on record. About thirty years ago, I was working for an IT company in Highbury, north London, as a technical writer. I liked the work and I also liked my work colleagues. These included the company's Top Brain and senior software architect, a likeable genius with a pleasantly eccentric nature and a rather Rasputin-like presence softened by a fondness for the silly side of life. He and I had completely different jobs but, due to a fluke of office desk allocation, worked more or less side by side and became good friends.

I once attended a fairly lively party at Top Brain's home. After the event had run its course and everyone else had left, I found myself having a chat with Top Brain in those dark, early morning hours when it feels good to talk about hopes, dreams and ideas. I was still a young man at the time so, unsurprisingly, my head was full of the type of ideas young men tend to have: a touch of admirable ambition spoiled by vagueness and shackled to the starting blocks by a naive and self-limiting lack of pragmatism.

For a while, as Rasputin changed the Steely Dan tracks playing quietly in the background, I rambled about my desire to perhaps one day work for myself. I said I'd quite like to try my hand at writing books. I also wondered if I could give talks on various subjects, perhaps incorporating a few touches of magic here and there for entertainment value. These musings were all from the 'castles in clouds' school of clueless perhaps-ism.

My friend listened with far greater interest than my words actually warranted. He then said, in his rather laid back, thoughtful manner, "I reckon if you had a go at that sort of thing, you'd do all right." He followed this up with a few reasons why he believed in my potential. It felt good to hear someone say they believed in me.

I know for a fact that those words of encouragement helped me to build the career that I wanted for myself. Don't get me wrong: I'm not claiming to be anyone's idea of an impressive success story. However, in my own entirely insignificant way, I've enjoyed my career and I'm glad I pursued the rather hazy, crazy ambitions I had at the time of that quiet conversation. I'd therefore like to thank the friend who said those words, and expressed his belief in me, all those years ago.

Thank you, JP Lodge.

- - -

I must add a strange note about this. When I first started working on this book, I settled on the name 'People Joy'. This was a very long time before I was working on this chapter and before it occurred to me to mention my old friend JP. I have said his kind remarks encouraged me to follow the path I've been on for the past 25-30 years. This path has culminated in this book — the title of which abbreviates to PJ.

From JP to PJ.

Have I moved forward through time or did time move backwards to me, in a reverse causality sort of way, and introduce me to JP? This is seriously rather weird.

Please Help Me If You Can

As we've now been together for over a hundred pages (doesn't time fly?!) I felt you wouldn't mind if I included this short request for help.

If you like this book, please encourage other people to buy a copy. My only sales team is you! Take the 'Two In Ten' challenge: see if, in the next ten days, you can persuade *two* people to buy this book.

You can also help me to publicise it. On my website, there's a page about good ways to do this:

www.ianrowland.com/peoplejoy/help

Tell everyone you know about 'People Joy' and suggest they buy a copy. Recommend this book in person, online and at work. Write a nice review on Amazon.

If you see a news item about people clashing, arguing and failing to communicate very well, you could refer to it on social media and say, 'Maybe they should read People Joy' and add a link to where people can buy this book!

People Joy is available from Amazon or directly from me: www.ianrowland.com

I sincerely appreciate any help you can give me.

— Ian

7. When You Talk: Mistakes To Avoid

"Too often we underestimate the power of a touch, a smile, a kind word, a listening ear, an honest compliment, or the smallest act of caring, all of which have the potential to turn a life around."

— Leo Buscaglia

Progress Check

In the last two chapters, I shared a few good ideas that will help you to have successful, transformative People Joy conversations.

In this chapter, I'm going to tell you about seven common mistakes that are well worth avoiding.

Part 1: Foundations

1. About Other People
2. About Yourself
3. About Conversations

Part 2: Talking

4. Before You Talk
5. When You Talk (1)
6. When You Talk (2)
7. When You Talk (3)
8. After You Talk

Part 3: Refinements

9. The Ten-second Smile
10. Voice Magic
11. More About Other People
12. More About You
13. The Joy Of Disagreement
14. Dealing With Anger

Part 4: Special Skills

15. The Art Of Selling
16. The Art Of Persuasion
17. The Art Of Cold Reading
18. Love Is What Works

1. Don't Hijack

Try not to be 'it's all about me'.

In this context, 'hijacking' means selfishly taking over someone else's conversational thread in a way that they find annoying.

Hijacking is the exact opposite of everything that People Joy is about. It's unkind, thoughtless and *never* leads to successful, happy and productive conversations. Quite the reverse. It suggests to the other person (OP) that you are only interested in 'me me me' conversations that are really just monologues. This is not a good impression to give to anyone. You may as well tell them, "You are insufficiently interesting for me to want to listen to you. I much prefer the sound of my own voice."

I need to make a fine distinction here. Suppose someone has shared their interesting story about, say, visiting the rather delightful city of Brighton. You have listened attentively and enjoyed the story. It's clear that the story has reached its natural conclusion. It's perfectly all right at this stage to offer *your* Brighton story as a way of naturally continuing the conversation and building on what the OP said. It's entirely different if someone is only part of the way through their story and you *interrupt* to say, "It's funny you should mention Brighton. A funny thing happened the last time I was there...".

Another form of hijacking involves switching the emotional focus of a conversation. Suppose you're talking to someone who feels they have been treated rather unfairly in a relationship. Clearly, they would welcome a bit of sympathy and emotional support. They would like to be listened to with some tactful understanding. If you ignore their situation and say, "I know what you mean. A similar thing happened to me once...", this is another example of unfortunate hijacking.

It's easy to make sure you never hijack a conversation. Before you launch into your own story, or offer your remarks, be sensitive to how the OP feels and ask yourself a few questions. Will they feel you're trying to be the centre of attention? Will they feel you always want the conversation to be about you and nobody else *but* you? Will they feel you're ignoring them instead of listening to what they want to say?

If the answer to any of these questions is yes, then don't say whatever you were going to say. Otherwise, go right ahead.

2. Don't Be A Two-Stepper

Want to be a social leper? Just become a two-stepper!

I have a friend called Fred who is *obsessed* with jazz music. If he's involved in *any* conversation, about *anything*, he always finds a way to bend the discussion round to jazz. It doesn't matter how tenuous or contrived the link is. He'll need two stepping stones, at most, to somehow get back to jazz music. In its own way, it's quite ingenious to see how he manages it.

Here are a few examples of what Fred sounds like.

Example #1

"Hi. I'd like to introduce Tony. He works at the British Museum and deals with ancient manuscripts."

Fred: "That's really important work, preserving our cultural heritage and so on. We feel the same way in the jazz world. It's important to preserve a lot of the old, early jazz recordings because..."

Example #2

"I've been on holiday in Italy. Turin, actually. Amazing place. I had a really great time."

Fred: "You know, we associate Italy with opera and classical music but they've produced some great jazz musicians as well. I recently got a couple of recordings by Marco Colonna and it's really great stuff..."

Example #3

"One of Sarah's friends organises sailing holidays on the south coast. We're getting a group together. Do you want to come?"

Fred: "I'd love to! You know, sailing is one of those things that looks a lot easier than it really is. It's the same in jazz. Improvising may look effortless on the surface but there's really a lot going on..."

This is what I mean by a two-stepper: someone who, given *any* subject, can always get back to their obsession in two steps at most. Don't be like this. Metaphorically, you're throwing a tin of blue paint over every conversation because you like the colour blue. This is against the spirit of People Joy because you're boring people rather than connecting with them and finding delight in them.

Maybe there's a particular cause or subject that you're passionate about. This is perfectly all right. However, don't assume other people want to hear about it *every* time they meet you. I promise that if people want to know about your pet subject, they'll ask you.

Incidentally, I don't *really* know a jazz enthusiast called Fred. He's imaginary. As it happens, I do know a few two-steppers in real life. However, I didn't think it would be fair to use them as an example here. They would be rather easy to identify within my social circle!

3. Validate Up, Not Down

The best validation involves elevation.

One way to get a bit of validation is to put other people down and point out how much better you are than them. It sounds like this:

> "Did you see John's presentation at the marketing meeting? He was awful and really boring. When I give a presentation like that I prepare much more thoroughly than he did. I remember to keep it short and allow time for questions."

> "I was round at Jane's house and saw how she talked to her five-year old. She hasn't a clue about parenting or what that child needs. When I raised my children, they were much happier and I knew how to give them confidence."

> "Did you see Fiona at the Magic Circle show on Friday? She only did two tricks and one of them went wrong. And she really left the audience cold. When I take part in those shows I work at a much better pace. Sometimes I even get a standing ovation."

This is known as *validating down*. You're giving yourself a few ego strokes by comparing yourself favourably to someone or something else. Even if you never actually say these things out loud, you might sometimes think them to yourself. You may as well wear a large sign saying, 'I didn't get enough validation when I was young and I've been trying to compensate ever since.'

Please don't *ever* do this. (1) It's a terrible way to get your validation. (2) You're creating a degree of suspicion about yourself. If you tell Alice bad things about Ben (who isn't present), she's likely to wonder what bad things you say about *her* when she's not around. (3) There is a much better way to get your validation. All you have to do is to *validate up*.

To see how this works, think what happens if you mention that you're friends with someone famous or a celebrity. People tend to be favourably impressed. You get a bit of reflected glory from the fact that you know this famous person. Since the celebrity is seen as cool, popular and successful, the fact that you know them suggests you must be a pretty impressive person too!

Validating up works in a similar way. Here are some examples of what it sounds like.

> "Did you see John give his presentation at the marketing meeting? He did really well. He was clear and got all his points across. Actually, we're working together on next month's regional campaign and it's going really well so far. We seem to make a good team and I'm pretty sure we're going to come in under budget."

> "I was round at Jane's house the other day and saw how her four-year old's coming along. I think Jane's really taken to motherhood. She sometimes asks me for a bit of advice plus we have a good laugh. I think she's turning out to be a good Mum and I'm glad I can help her out here and there."

> "Did you see Fiona's performance on Friday at the Magic Circle show? I thought she was excellent and her act was highly creative. Actually, we're meeting up soon to plan her competition act. We tend to come up with some good ideas when we work together."

Validating up involves a simple pattern.

1. That person is great (for some reason).

2. I'm associated with them.

3. It follows by implication that I must be pretty great too.

Validating up is far more effective than validating down. Every time you validate up, you're training yourself to see the best in people and to admire their good points rather than their bad ones. This is a vital aspect of People Joy. Also, you create an aura around yourself as someone who prefers to say positive things about other people. Over time, people will notice that you're generous with your praise, respect and admiration.

Validating down is a *terrible* idea and far more destructive than you might think. As ideas go, it's about as much use as a prickly pillow. Validating up is a far more successful strategy *and* helps you to maintain your self-greatness.

4. The Snow White Principle

No one cares how Snow White's grandparents met.

A lot of people who have a good story to share make the mistake of starting too far back. They wade through all sorts of rather dull and irrelevant details before getting to the part that the other person will find interesting, fun or relevant. This is like telling the story of Snow White and starting off with how her grandparents met.

Mentally edit your stories or whatever you want to share with the OP. Choose a good starting point that doesn't involve them sitting through fifteen minutes of yawn for one moment of interest. There are ways to get to the good part faster. You can use short introductory phrases such as, "For context, just let me explain that...", or, "For this story, you only need to know two things.....", and then quickly sketch in a bit of background. This conveys your respect for the other person's time and attention.

Don't start with Snow White's grandparents!

(There are a few places in this book where I have shared stories and anecdotes. Feel free to write and tell me that I started the stories too far back and thereby failed to take my own advice. For that matter, you may want to tell me that the whole book is flabby and long-winded. I'll be happy to agree with you. No one who knows me well has ever mistaken me for a shining beacon of perfection. As I say elsewhere, a good idea remains a good idea even if I personally fail to implement it.)

5. The Bicycle Principle

What's clear brings cheer. Clarity is charity.

If you come along to The Magic Circle clubroom one evening, you might well hear one of my magician friends say, "I tried using bicycles for a while but these days I prefer bees."

On the surface, this sounds like gibberish. In what possible context could someone 'use' bees or say they prefer a bee to a bicycle? However, to anyone else in the clubroom this would make perfect sense. As it happens, Bee and Bicycle are two different brands of playing cards. My magician friend is simply explaining that she prefers one brand to the other.

For People Joy purposes, make sure your conversations are *inclusive* rather than *exclusive*. Don't use opaque jargon or references that the person you're talking to won't understand. It's inconsiderate and an excellent way to waste what could have been a good conversation. Instead of connecting with someone, you'll leave them baffled and bewildered. Trade jargon is fine for people who can understand it. For everyone else, it's a barrier to comprehension.

It's also worth bearing this point in mind during group conversations. Don't let anyone feel left behind because the rest of you are using terms and references they don't understand.

6. The Tuning Principle

Match your expression to the session.

Learn to 'tune in' to the people you're talking to and express yourself appropriately. This involves being aware of people's sensitivities, limitations and boundaries. For example, some people enjoy vulgar and risqué humour. Others really find it distasteful and juvenile. Some people don't mind in the slightest if you use swear words and coarse language. Other people really *don't* like it and will probably decide you're not someone they want to talk to. They may also feel you have a poor vocabulary and can't express yourself very well.

Tune in to how other people express themselves. Adjust the tone and manner of your conversation so that you and the other person can *both* enjoy it. This isn't hard to do.

There's a lot of discussion these days about people being too easily 'offended'. This book isn't about the rights and wrongs of people alleging that a comedy routine was offensive. It's about having successful, transformative conversations that lead to good things for you and everyone you talk to. If you use language, humour or ways of expressing yourself that the other person doesn't like or can't enjoy, you're not having the best conversation you could have. It's exclusive rather than inclusive and not a good People Joy thing to do.

7. Shine, Don't Preach

Preachy isn't peachy.

If you're with a group of people who all share the same faith, politics or ideology, where preaching is *expected* and *welcome*, then preaching is perfectly fine. In all other situations, sounding 'preachy' is a bad move. You will rapidly achieve the opposite of everything People Joy is about. Also, you won't inspire anyone to do anything except try to get away from you.

Sounding preachy is a waste of time. In the context of a normal, everyday conversation, there is no instance in history of someone listening to a lengthy, preachy rant and feeling moved to support whatever the preachy person is advocating. "Wow, tell me more and where do I sign up?!" is not how this ends.

If you really want to get people interested in your cause, ideology or way of life, there's far better option that you can pursue. It doesn't annoy anyone and stands a very good chance of winning people over to your cause or personal beliefs. All you have to do is *shine*. In other words, if you're someone's neighbour, try to be a really superb, helpful, friendly neighbour. If you're someone's work colleague, be someone they enjoy working with and love having around. If you're someone's friend, be a great and valued friend whom they know they can always count on.

Whatever role you play in someone's life, play it so well that you consistently make a good impression on them. Don't be afraid to impress to excess! Enjoy setting yourself the happy challenge of being the best neighbour, colleague, friend (or whatever) that you can be. In the fullness of time, the people around you might feel sufficiently impressed or inspired by you to ask about your outlook, values and way of life. They might think to themselves, "I don't know what [your name]'s got, but whatever it is, I want some of it."

That's the time to share your beliefs, principles, ideology or way of life with people. Not before.

Don't *preach*. It's boring, counter-productive and repels people. It's the opposite of what People Joy is all about.

Aim to *shine*, so that people ask you where the light comes from. As Shakespeare puts it so well:

> *"While fools attempt a laboured advocation*
> *Made of a scoundrel's din that grates and grinds*
> *The wiser heart plies good, kind demonstration*
> *As route to loyal track of hearts and minds."*
> (Coriolanus, Act III, scene ii)

Chapter Summary

Here are the seven mistakes I mentioned in this chapter:

- Don't hijack.

- Don't be a two-stepper.

- Validate up, not down.

- The Snow White principle.

- The bicycle principle.

- The tuning principle.

- Shine, don't preach.

To echo what I said at the end of the 'Snow White' part, I'm sure I make all these mistakes on a regular basis. I thought I'd point this out to save anyone else the trouble (such as *all my friends* and *everyone who knows me*). I'm trying to pass along a few good ideas, not claiming to be a peerless paragon of personal perfection.

DUCK

The Taxi Driver's Tale

I first heard about 'shine, don't preach' about twenty years ago. I was taking a ride in a taxi. The driver was a young man, perhaps in his early thirties, who happened to be Sikh. We got talking about his background, where his family came from in India and his religious beliefs. He mentioned that, in the Sikh religion, they don't believe in preaching. In fact, he was rather humorously dismissive of the whole idea. "It's so boring," he said, briefly mimicking preachy behaviour. "Nobody wants that all the time."

He told me that rather than preaching, the Sikh way was to live your life so that you're a good advert for your faith. If you're someone's neighbour, be a great neighbour. Someone's work colleague? Be a great work colleague… and so on. "That's the way we do it," said the taxi driver. "Eventually, people might start thinking, 'I don't know what he's got, but I want some of it'. Then, if they ask, we can explain what Sikhism is all about." I thought this was a fascinating conversation and it stayed with me.

I am not saying this is necessarily an accurate summary of Sikh attitudes or one that all followers of Sikhism would agree with. I'm simply sharing something a taxi driver told me. Nonetheless, I think he was making a valuable point.

Baffling Terminology

I mentioned that both 'Bicycle' and 'Bee' are brands of playing cards. Many magicians use 'Bicycle' cards simply because they're good quality, reasonably priced and handle well. (I've been bribed quite substantially to say this. The 'Bee' marketing department should have submitted a higher offer.)

Sometimes, we refer to these cards as 'bikes', because obviously it's too much effort to pronounce 'Bicycle' in its entirety. Also, we tend to buy these decks of cards in boxes of 12, informally known in the trade as 'bricks'. Hence you might hear one magician casually say to another, "I'm going to buy a brick of bikes". It's truly a world of curious terminology.

While writing this chapter, I asked my friends for further examples of specialist trade jargon where familiar words play unfamiliar roles. Here's a selection.

Casinos and gambling. "The dealer polished her shoe while in the pit under the eye in the sky." (She made sure the device she deals cards from was working smoothly, while on the floor where the card games take place, underneath the security camera in the ceiling.)

IT and network security. "That box has been popped. Is the canary okay?'" (The computer or server has been compromised by a hacker. Is the program that periodically tests that the service is still working normally saying everything is okay?)

Home brewing. "I'm going to measure the gravity and rack off'. (I'm going to measure the relative density of the beer/wine to assess its alcohol content and then transfer it from one container to another, leaving behind the yeast sediment.)

Retail computer sales. "I need a 'mickey mouse' for a PSU." (I need a round 3-pin power lead for a computer/laptop power supply unit.)

Marketing. "I was in the Cat Man meeting." (I was in a meeting with the Category Management team.)

Circus skills. "I tried to free-mount a giraffe." (I tried to climb up on to a very tall unicycle without any aid or support.)

Skydiving. "I put on a rig to go to altitude and lob but there was cloud and I missed the sucker hole so I had to do a hop and pop." (I put on my parachute to go up and do a jump. It was a cloudy day but there was one patch of clear blue sky. However, by the time I was ready the cloud base was low and so I had to jump out of the plane and deploy my canopy right away.)

Skateboarding. "He just switch backlipped the hubba!". (He slid down the hubba, meaning an architectural ledge that runs diagonally downwards alongside a set of steps in place of a handrail. This is named after Hubba Hideout, a famous skate spot that had a ledge of this type and was so called because 'hubba' is slang for crack cocaine and the area was reputed to be a hangout for addicts. It became so famous among skateboarders that every such ledge worldwide came to be called a 'Hubba'. He performed his move in such a way that his back wheels were on top of the ledge and he was facing away from the bottom of the steps as he slid down them — which is called a backlip, being short for 'backside lipslide'.)

8. After You Talk

"A conversation is so much more than words: a conversation is eyes, smiles, the silences between the words."

— Annika Thor

Progress Check

So far, in Part Two of this book, we've had chapters about *before* you talk, *when* you talk and some mistakes to avoid.

In this final chapter of Part Two, I'd like to share a few ideas about what to do *after* a conversation.

Part 1: Foundations

1. About Other People
2. About Yourself
3. About Conversations

Part 2: Talking

4. Before You Talk
5. When You Talk (1)
6. When You Talk (2)
7. When You Talk (3)
8. After You Talk

Part 3: Refinements

9. The Ten-second Smile
10. Voice Magic
11. More About Other People
12. More About You
13. The Joy Of Disagreement
14. Dealing With Anger

Part 4: Special Skills

15. The Art Of Selling
16. The Art Of Persuasion
17. The Art Of Cold Reading
18. Love Is What Works

The Game Of Small Favours

Let's say you've enjoyed a good conversation with someone. You want to stay in touch and build a mutually beneficial relationship. This could be for personal, social or business reasons. A good way to do this is to play the game of small favours. During the conversation, make a mental note of *any* opportunity to do a small favour for the other person (OP) after the conversation.

It doesn't really matter what the favour happens to be. The point is to demonstrate that you *enjoyed* the conversation, you were *paying attention* and you're a *thoughtful* person. Perhaps you could send the OP a funny cartoon or an article relevant to your discussion, or some useful follow-up information. Maybe you can introduce the OP to a friend who can help with a problem they mentioned.

You can also follow up conversations by sending someone a small gift, such as a book, some flowers or something practical. Thanks to Amazon and other online retailers, it's never been easier, quicker or cheaper to send someone a small gift. Don't try to impress the OP with your wealth or generosity. Your thoughtfulness is what matters, not the cash value of the gift. You are doing them a small favour that provides *tangible* evidence that you'd like to keep in touch.

In life, and in business, giving is a *great* way to win.

Shock And Awe

Here's a slight variation on the game of small favours. My friend Charlie Hutton runs the 'One Man Empire' business group for entrepreneurs. He once invited me to lecture to his group on persuasion and cold reading and it was a hugely enjoyable day.

Charlie, together with Emma Hutchinson, wrote a superb business book called 'The Orgasm Effect', which I highly recommend. They mention the concept of a 'Shock And Awe' box, so called because it makes such a strong, favourable impression on people. They cite the example of an estate agent (realtor) who, once people have moved into their new home, sends them a box containing a few practical items and treats. Each box costs the estate agent about £30 but pays for itself many times over in terms of favourable referrals. Many businesses might like to consider doing something similar.

HEART Gifts

This is one of the greatest People Joy secrets I can share with you. Please do not overlook this idea. You won't find it in any business book but it's an idea that works so well it's close to real magic.

As before, let's say you've enjoyed a conversation with someone and you'd like to follow it up in a likeable, thoughtful way that makes a good impression. You also want to make sure the OP remembers you in a positive way. I can tell you the *greatest* way to do this. It *always* works and in fact it can't fail to work. It's an idea I have loved using for over thirty years. If you want to build and sustain excellent connections with people, *this* is absolutely the finest and most effective way to do it.

Here's the idea: send the other person a HEART gift.

'HEART' stands for Handmade, Exceptional, Appropriate, Remarkable and Tailored.

A HEART gift is one that *money can't buy*. It's something you *make* for the person you want to stay in touch with. It's exceptional in the sense of being unique and something no one else could send to them. It's also 'tailored' or customised in that it can feature the recipient's name or initials.

Over the years, I've sent people three types of HEART gifts. Let's take a quick jog through them.

Sonnet

My first example of a HEART gift is an acrostic sonnet. For the benefit of anyone who has better things to do than remember this stuff, or who has a life, a sonnet is a poem consisting of 14 lines that has to follow a specific rhyme scheme. 'Acrostic' means the first letters of each line spell out a name or message.

For example, I'm fortunate enough to include bestselling author Isabel Losada among my friends. She writes superb books that everyone should read and enjoy (see this chapter's DUCK for more details). One year, I was invited to Isabel's birthday party so, by way of a gift, I wrote an acrostic sonnet for her. There are only 12 letters in her name, rather than 14, so for the first two lines I used the letters 'HB' for 'Happy Birthday'. If you only read the first letters of each line they spell 'HB Isabel Losada'.

Upon The Occasion Of Isabel's Birthday

Her gifted prose, composed of sense and quirk
Brings light and wit both welcome in this world
In that we need both more, and in her work
See both well-wrought, and stylishly unfurled

All muses do attend and bless her arts
By turns she writes, she acts, she sings sublime
Each mode one hue within her rainbow heart's
Lust to express and scope the soul divine

Long may she celebrate her gift of life
Of sorrows few, of love and laughter more
Success to be her star, not storm or strife
And inner peace her constant, sun-baked shore

Drink then a toast, long may her karma guard her
An Amazonian Queen, Lady Losada!

The hardest part, as you can imagine, was finding anything to rhyme with Isabel's surname!

Tessellation Scribbles

Here's another example of a type of HEART gift that I send to people. In the Introduction's DUCK, I mentioned that I make 'tessellations', or patterns based on a repeated figure that slots together with itself in a (hopefully) pleasant and intriguing fashion. Some people like them.

I sometimes make one of these designs as a HEART gift. The recipient can choose the hues and colours they'd like me to use. I create the design and get a high-resolution print made on art paper, either A4 or A3 size, which I send out in a poster tube.

Here are some examples. They look better in colour, obviously, as you can see on my website (ianrowland.com/peoplejoy). Below is an abstract design I made for a friend (no personalisation) and the single tile it's made from. On the opposite page is a design I made for a friend whose initials are 'BC' and another for a couple I know whose first names begin with 'M' and 'S'.

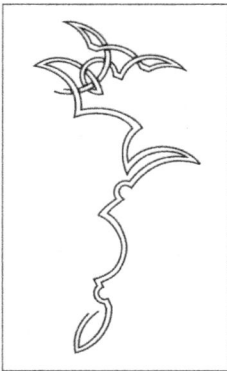

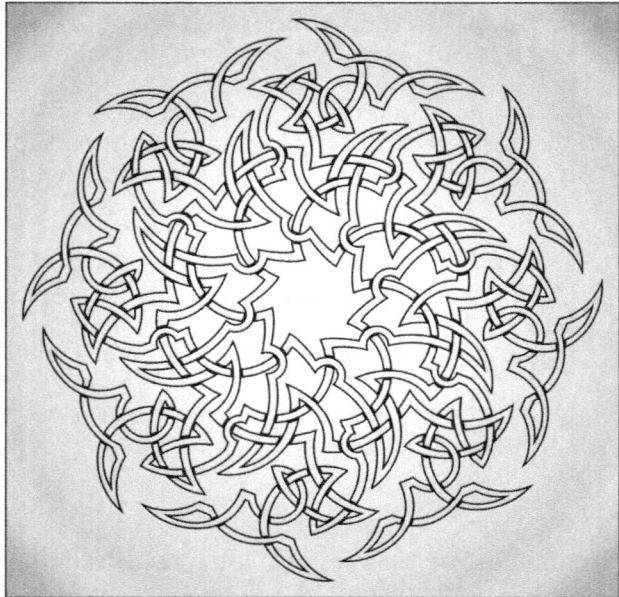

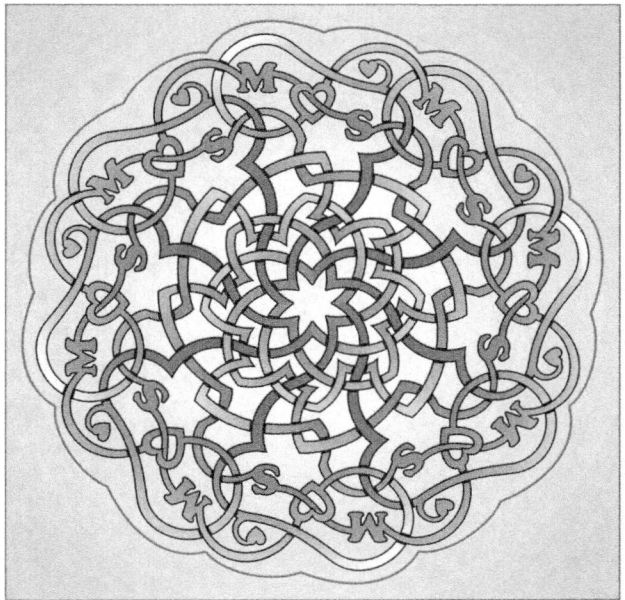

Ian Cards

Here's my third and final example of a HEART gift I sometimes make for people. I take a playing card, make a few slits and folds and end up with something like the example you see here. This process, which is technically known as 'kirigami', does not involve glue or adhesive. Nothing has been cut and then glued back together. If you wanted to, you could unfold the card back to its initial, flat state.

Over the years I've created many different Ian Card designs. This particular design can be customised to feature any two initials. I make the card and then send it to the recipient on its own or in a perspex clip frame for display purposes. If it's near Valentine's Day, and I'm making the card for someone to give to their partner, I can make it from the Two of Hearts, just for an extra romantic touch.

This form of card 'sculpture' was pioneered by my friend Angus Lavery (see the DUCK for more information).

What Will Yours Be?

Giving someone a HEART gift *guarantees* that they'll smile and remember you in a favourable way. I don't know how many HEART gifts I've made for people over the years but I know it's a lot. People tell me they *love* them. The fact that what they receive is clearly *not* something money can buy makes the recipient feel special.

It's worth thinking about the type of HEART gift *you* could give to people. Obviously, this depends on your creative talents, interests and abilities. The gift doesn't have to be a tangible object. For example, I know some talented singers and musicians who can create any music they want, from songs to film scores, in their home studio. Some of them create HEART gifts in the form of, say, a short song or musical snippet that they can send to the recipient as an audio file.

You might say you have no creative talents. Please don't undermine your self-greatness in this way. It is almost certainly the case that you haven't so far had the *opportunity* or inclination to explore your creative potential. I feel confident you could devise your own HEART gift if you really wanted to.

If you seriously believe you can't come up with a HEART gift yourself, all is not lost. You can ask someone else to make your HEART gifts for you! There are literally thousands of creative people offering their goods and services all over the internet. It's fun to spend a bit of time exploring Etsy and similar websites. Whatever you'd like to send out as a HEART gift, you'll be able to find someone willing to make it!

I'm lucky enough to count numerous creative and talented people among my friends. Many of them make unique items of the type that you could send as HEART gifts. I've shared three examples on the next couple of pages but I could have included many more.

You'll find contact information for everyone I mention in this chapter on my website: ianrowland.com/peoplejoy.

My talented friend Jayne Corrigan is a magician, artist and many other things besides. She makes 'Corrigami' books like the one you see here. Starting with an old book, she patiently folds back the pages to create a name or set of initials.

These books are mesmerising. Jayne kindly made this one for me and I've proudly displayed it on my shelves for years.

My dear friend Barbara Mervine makes cute, felted-wool creatures such as this sheep and magic rabbit. They are unique and adorable.

Many years ago, I attended the 'Gathering For Gardner' convention, which celebrates the work and legacy of Martin Gardner. His 'Mathematical Games' columns in 'Scientific American' had a profound influence on me. At the convention, I met Chris Palmer, who describes himself as a designer, geometer and ornamentalist folder! He creates amazing, intricate, geometrically-based origami. Chris kindly gave me a couple of examples of his work. His 'business card' unfolds beautifully as shown.

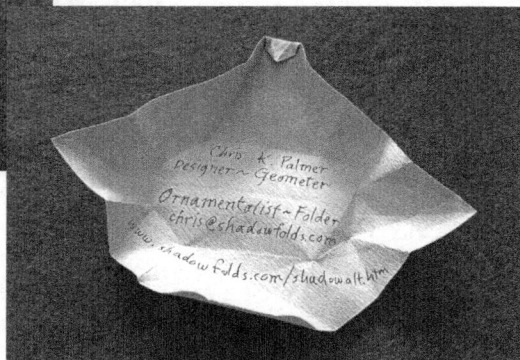

The Value Of HEART Gifts

It's worth taking a moment to consider why HEART gifts are so effective. Let's say you met someone, you had a great conversation and now you'd like to be *unforgettable* in that person's eyes. There are two aspects of being unforgettable: you have to be *exceptional* and you have to somehow achieve an *enduring* presence in their mind and memory.

A HEART gift achieves both of these aims. They are exceptional by definition, since they are unique and *not* mass-produced. They are also enduring because people like to keep them around in their office, workplace or home. Some of my friends and clients have had one of my HEART gifts for twenty or thirty years.

If you work in sales, especially business-to-business sales, you're constantly searching for ways to differentiate yourself from the competition. Let's say you'd like to win a large order from Company XYZ. The chief buyer at XYZ sees a hundred people like you every year. She's seen so many brochures, presentations and sales pitches that they are all just a blur. How do you stand out from the crowd? Clearly, sending a HEART gift is one way to do it. You can't send HEART gifts to the thousands of clients and prospects on your database. However, you could send them to a few, carefully selected people you *really* want to impress.

Chapter Summary

This chapter was about things you can do after a conversation to enhance the conversation's legacy. The three main ideas were:

- The game of small favours.

- Shock and awe.

- HEART gifts.

This brings Part Two of this book to an end. We looked at good People Joy techniques to use *before* you talk, *when* you talk and *after* you talk to people. In Part Three, I'll share some refinements to the ideas I've mentioned so far in this book.

DUCK

Isabel Losada

My friend Isabel Losada is a best-selling author who has written several superb books that you should all read. My own personal favourites include 'The Battersea Park Road to Enlightenment' and 'The Joyful Environmentalist', the latter being enjoyably *non*-preachy in tone. I strongly recommend that you check out her work. You will not be disappointed. In addition, if you *ever* get the chance to meet Isabel in person, for example at one of her book signings or a live event, I suggest you take the opportunity. She's effervescently bright, charming, smart, engaging and funny.

Angus Lavery

In this chapter I mentioned taking a playing card and making some slits and folds in it to create an intriguing pattern — one that can also include someone's initials. As far as I know, the first person to magically transform playing cards in this way was my friend Angus Lavery. Many years ago, he kindly shared some of his techniques with me to get me started. Angus was once the resident 'puzzle expert' at the famous Hamley's toy shop in London. He has an amazing mind and his card creations are simply extraordinary.

Not Art

I wish to make it clear that, in my opinion, none of the things I make for people constitute 'art'. Not that it matters, but I thought I'd point this out to save anyone else the trouble of doing so. On one or two occasions, people who *are* artists have been keen to let me know that I am *not* one. To save time, I thought I should mention that I agree.

I am not an artist. My brain is wired up to process words and semantic data (to a truly ridiculous extent) but can barely handle visual data at all. I apparently have a condition called 'aphantasia', which means I don't have the same mental cinema screen as most people. Asking me to visualise something is a bit unfair, like asking a cow to fly. All the same, I enjoy dabbling with tessellations and similar scribbles.

If don't think my opinion about this matters but if anyone happens to want it then here it is.

'The Hay Wain' by John Constable is art.

'Self-Portrait' from 1659, by Rembrandt van Rijn, is art.

'Ascending And Descending' by M.C. Escher, the artist who changed my life, is art.

'The Hunters In The Snow', by Pieter Bruegel the Elder, is art. This is probably my favourite painting and I was lucky enough to see it when I visited the magnificent Kunsthistorisches Museum in Vienna.

'Nighthawks' by Edward Hopper is art.

'Home For Thanksgiving' and 'The Shiner / Girl With Black Eye' by Norman Rockwell are art.

Bearing these examples in mind, I would feel that I was being ridiculously pretentious if I used the word 'art' to describe anything I know how to make. This is just my opinion.

Part Three: Refinements

9. The Ten-Second Smile

*"The best way to cheer yourself is
to try to cheer someone else up."*

— Mark Twain

Progress Check

Part One of this book was about the three foundations of People Joy.

Part Two was about good People Joy ideas you can use before, during and after conversations.

This brings us to Part Three of this book, which as you can see I've called 'Refinements'. I'm going to explore six further aspects of successful and effective conversations.

To start this section, I want to share one of my favourite aspects of People Joy. It's an idea that will make a profound, positive difference to the way you talk to people for the rest of your life. It's also fun to know about and to use.

Part 1: Foundations

1. About Other People
2. About Yourself
3. About Conversations

Part 2: Talking

4. Before You Talk
5. When You Talk (1)
6. When You Talk (2)
7. When You Talk (3)
8. After You Talk

Part 3: Refinements

9. The Ten-second Smile
10. Voice Magic
11. More About Other People
12. More About You
13. The Joy Of Disagreement
14. Dealing With Anger

Part 4: Special Skills

15. The Art Of Selling
16. The Art Of Persuasion
17. The Art Of Cold Reading
18. Love Is What Works

A Transformative Skill

This chapter is all about a technique called the ten-second smile. This is one of the greatest ideas that I can share with you. Looking back over the years, I have no doubt that this technique has changed my life for the better in countless ways. I hope it will do the same for you.

If you want to be successful, you need to know about this technique. If you want to know how to sell and persuade, or how to have a richer, happier life, or how to make the world a better place, you need to know about this technique.

What I am going to describe is a skill. Like any other skill, it will come more easily to some people than others. However, even if you struggle to master it at first, I urge you not to give up. It will change your life and deliver countless benefits.

Getting Started

Here's the basic idea. Whenever you meet someone or start a conversation, mentally set yourself a small challenge. Aim to make the other person (OP) *smile* or *laugh* within the first ten seconds of the conversation. That's all there is to it. You set yourself this private challenge of causing one more smile or laugh to appear in the world than there was before.

Here's the golden rule: you have to do this in a way that the OP *likes* and *enjoys*. You have failed if the OP finds it annoying, stupid, inappropriate, tiresome or inconvenient.

Like all the ideas in this book, you obviously have to use this technique sensitively and with a bit of common sense. Don't use the ten-second smile when it would be crass or inappropriate.

There are two flavours of the ten-second smile (TSS):

- Simple. This means using the TSS *without* intending to be funny or amusing.

- Humorous. Using the TSS and intending to be funny or at least mildly humorous.

The Simple TSS

This version of the ten-second smile does *not* involve trying to be amusing or humorous. Instead, you aim to elicit the smile reflex just by saying something kind, pleasant, helpful, relatable or appreciative.

Let's consider a few ways to do this.

One good option is simply to mention something that you and the OP have in common. There was a section about this in Chapter 5, 'Signs of Sameness'. I mentioned four common subjects that can often provide a point of connection: Likes and dislikes, Employment, Geography and Story (which you can remember as 'LEGS').

Another excellent path to a simple TSS just involves offering a sincere compliment. It must be one the OP will appreciate and *not* consider unwelcome or inappropriate.

Perhaps one of the best paths to a simple TSS is to offer thanks, credit or acknowledgement. Everyone enjoys a touch of genuine gratitude and appreciation once in a while. Imagine you're in a coffee shop with friends and a waitress brings you the snack you ordered. You could say something like this:

> "Thank you. Can I just say something? This place gets really busy and I expect your job's quite tiring at times — I know I'd be worn out after ten minutes! But you always provide really good, efficient service. Thank you. We appreciate it."

If you say something like this with genuine warmth and respect, you're likely to elicit a smile. Mission accomplished!

Offering someone a bit of help is another good way to achieve a simple TSS. There are always opportunities to perform acts of practical kindness if you look for them:

> "Would you like some help carrying that suitcase up the steps? / Would you like me to reach that top shelf for you? / You look like you're in more of a hurry than I am — do you want to go ahead of me in the queue?"

Yet another path towards a simple TSS is to ask someone a question in a friendly way and then thank them for their help.

"Excuse me, do you know if there's a café round here where I can get a coffee?" [They answer the question.] "Thank you! I appreciate your help."

It doesn't really matter *how* you make the other person smile. So long as they smile, you've won. Well done! The sum total of smiles in the world just went up by one. Maybe you could set yourself a small daily target. See if you can create three smiles, every single day. Imagine what the world would be like if we all tried to create smiles instead of finding ways to dislike one another.

Humorous TSS

This version of the ten-second smile involves trying to be funny, humorous or at least mildly amusing.

I am *not* saying you should act like a clown or try to be a comedian. Also, I am *not* suggesting you should memorise lots of feeble jokes. Instead, aim to say something friendly and amusing about the *situation* in which you and the OP find yourselves. In other words, something amusing about your *current shared experience*.

This approach makes it clear to the OP that you are *not* just reciting stale jokes. It shows that you have a sufficiently active mind to have noticed something amusing in your immediate environment. This approach also guarantees that whatever you say will be *relatable*. Relatable things, by definition, bring people together.

When you use the humorous TSS, always make sure it's *inclusive* humour rather than *exclusive*. Exclusive humour involves regarding certain people or groups as the *victim* of the joke, to be mocked and vilified. Inclusive humour doesn't involve any victims. It proceeds from the attitude that life's a little crazy and sometimes difficult, we're all just trying our best so let's help one another and share a few laughs along the way. It's humour that *everyone* can enjoy and that brings people together rather than pushing them apart.

This flavour of the ten-second smile involves a subtle degree of respect. In effect, you are saying to the OP, "I think you are sufficiently smart to recognise that I'm sharing some fun with you. You can join in if you want." It's a wonderful thing to make someone laugh and *also* convey the fact that you respect them.

Finding The Fun: TSS Cues

How can you find humorous things to say to people around you that will elicit a little laughter?

You may be the sort of person who finds this quite easy to do. If not, let me try to offer some help. The general aim is to notice strange, odd and absurd aspects of life that you can mention to whoever you're with. In essence, you are looking for signs of the richness of human error and fallibility. This tends to come in two main flavours.

The first is that every system devised by the human mind is *supposed* to work perfectly but never does. As a species, we're much better at theory than we are at practice. All software has bugs in it, *every* procedural policy has holes and every 'plan that can't fail' will at some point be defeated by human error. The world is full of 'Lost Property' offices that are closed because the person in charge has lost the key.

The second point, related to the first, is that there is always a gulf between *representation* and *reality*. Stories, promises and glossy pictures are easy. Living up to them is hard. If you look online you can find collections comparing attractive holiday brochure photos with what you get in reality.

Here are nine cue words that will help you to achieve a Humorous TSS. They are all paths to amusing, *relatable* things you can share with whoever you happen to be with:

- Place, Prop, Problem.

- Sense, Similar, Sound.

- Want, Wear, Words.

Whenever you want to say something amusing to someone, based on your *current shared experience*, mentally flip through these nine cues. With a little practice, I'm sure you'll find something amusing to say.

In the following sections, I mention examples of how I've applied these cues in the past. It's all right if you think these examples are as funny as cardboard. As we all know, humour is highly subjective and often subject to context. I'm not trying to dazzle you with my wit. I'm just trying to show how you can use these cues in real life.

Place

Look around at the place or location in which you and the OP find yourselves. Can you *see* anything amusing about it? Is there anything you wouldn't have expected or that indicates unfulfilled aspirations? Bear in mind that 'place' could refer to the town you're in, or this particular part of town, or this street, or the coffee shop you're visiting. You decide how far to zoom in or zoom out, mentally speaking.

Look around for evidence of the two aspects of life I mentioned: flaws in human behaviour and systems or the typical human instinct to represent things as being slightly better than they really are.

Real-life example. I was once speaking at a conference in Arad, Romania. Everyone at the conference stayed in the same luxurious 'high class' hotel. It was perfect in every way — except the corridors featured the ugliest carpeting I've ever seen. When I saw it for the first time, I *honestly* thought there had been an accident involving spillage of industrial solvents! It was strange that this beautiful hotel had such ugly carpets everywhere. I took some photos and later, when talking to delegates, this dreadful carpeting was one of my paths to a TSS. We all agreed it could actually make you feel unwell!

Prop

In TV and films, a 'prop' (short for 'property') is any physical item that the characters use or handle. I'm using this term in the same way. Always notice the things people are using, carrying or have lying around. They can often provide material for a TSS.

Real-life example. I was once checking in to a hotel in Lisbon and enjoying a chat with the receptionist, who wasn't very busy at the time. On her desk was the biggest, heaviest, most massive 'long arm' stapler I've ever seen. It looked like it weighed half a ton. I gestured towards it and said, "Wow! You could actually kill someone with that. Is that what you hit customers over the head with if they misbehave? I'm scared now. I promise to be a good guest."

The receptionist laughed a little. Leaning towards me in a sly, conspiratorial manner, she admitted that yes, she occasionally used this massive stapler in this way. However, she assured me she tried not to resort to this tactic *too* often — only on guests she *really* didn't like. She thanked me for promising to be a *good* guest.

Problem

Problems are fertile ground for laughter because they are an inescapable part of human experience. To be human is to witness things going wrong. We constantly strive for greatness only to be betrayed by the 'idiot' circuits in our heads. When you're searching for something amusing to talk about, look for signs of problems worth commenting on. Are there systems in place that don't work? Where is the gap between noble aspirations and dismal, flawed reality?

Real-life example. During a visit to Miami, I took one of the excellent airboat tours around the Everglades. The sales literature suggested we'd see plenty of local wildlife, the star attraction being the alligators native to the region. The tour went well. However, it soon became clear that the poor guy driving the boat couldn't find any alligators no matter how hard he tried! This led to heated exchanges between the hapless driver and one or two disgruntled passengers.

"You promised us alligators!"

"I know, but they're wild animals, right? We can't just tell them to appear. I'm doing my best to find one for you."

"There's even alligators on the posters."

"I *know* what's on the posters. But they do say we can't *guarantee* what you'll see."

"I want my money back. This is a ripoff."

"No one's trying to rip you off. They're wild animals. Believe me, I'm trying my best."

This saga of implacable protest may not sound all that amusing. Nonetheless, it was highly entertaining at the time. I got more than one TSS out of the situation, both when chatting with other (more reasonable) passengers on the boat itself and afterwards with friends. I loved the idea of an entire industry built around *one* main attraction — alligators! — having to contend with the *slight* problem of not being able to find any. It reminded me of the famous Monty Python 'cheese shop' sketch. By the way, the Everglades tours are thoroughly enjoyable and I highly recommend them. The one I was on was just unlucky (and we did *eventually* see some alligators).

Sense

Look around you for things that defy reason or simply don't make sense. I doubt you'll have to look for very long. As I've mentioned, *every* human system works less than perfectly. It pays to keep an eye out for the crazy side of life and things that seem notably bereft of sense or reason.

Real-life example. I once visited Hawaii with my girlfriend-at-the-time. While exploring Big Island, following one of the official trails on the map, we came across a sign as big as the side of a house. This scary, imposing sign declared that we were strictly *forbidden* from proceeding any further along the trail. It said there had been a volcanic eruption, there was molten lava in the area and we had to turn back for our own safety. As we meekly complied, we met two locals. They cheerfully informed us that it was safe to ignore the sign. They explained that it had been put up *twelve years ago*, during an emergency, but was now irrelevant.

This didn't make any sense. Why, in twelve years, had no one taken down this huge, misleading, unhelpfully *scary* sign? It also seemed obvious that, sooner or later, leaving the sign up was certain to lead to a tragic 'boy who cried wolf' scenario. I got several TSS moments out of this experience while I was in Hawaii. (I have no idea if the sign is *still* there but I'd love to know!)

On the subject of things that don't make sense, anyone visiting a foreign country will find some intriguing cultural differences. In Italy, if you want to buy a bus ticket, you go to a *tobacconist*. Why? I've no idea. Do they get their cigarettes from a bus? Then again, Italians who visit England find it puzzling (and faintly disgusting) that we have washing machines in the kitchen. I'm told they also find it odd that we don't have siestas or take long lunches. Every culture is an enigma to those unaccustomed to it. As Shakespeare expresses it so well:

> *"The common stock of our familiar ways*
> *That constitute our reputation's core*
> *May yet beguile, bewilder and amaze*
> *The witness from a distant, far-off shore"*
> (Cymbeline, Act III, scene ii)

Similar

Similarity, or the *lack* of similarity, can also lead to a good TSS. Does someone you've met remind you of someone else? Perhaps you expected the place you're in to be similar to a place you know and you're either pleased or disappointed to find that it isn't.

Real-life example. I mentioned that a distinct *lack* of similarity can provide the path to a TSS. I live in London, a hugely impressive city with a rich cultural and historical heritage. There's plenty to see and enjoy and you should all come and pay a visit. Unfortunately, we're just not very good at keeping it clean. There's dirt, litter and graffiti everywhere (especially near the signs that say 'No littering!').

For this reason, I experienced a significant culture shock when I visited Tokyo, where they do things slightly differently. Every single morning, a small army of young people, in smart blue uniforms and white gloves, work their way across the city and clean it with meticulous efficiency! They clear away rubbish, hose the pavements, wash the walls and generally keep everywhere looking clean and tidy. The stark contrast in civic pride between this and my home city gave me an easy path to a TSS when talking to my Japanese hosts and friends.

Sound

Open your ears and pay attention to what you can *hear*. Maybe there will be something that could lead to a humorous TSS.

Real-life example. I once visited the magnificent city of Buenos Aires. As many tourists do, I visited La Recoleta Cemetery to see Eva Peron's tomb. It bears her maiden name, 'Duarte' — a fact made quite clear by various signs in Spanish and English. There was a guide standing near the main entrance. I don't speak Spanish but I could tell that almost everyone who approached him was asking exactly the same question and he had to give exactly the same answer:

"¿Dónde está Eva Perón?"

"Buscá el apellido Duarte, por ahí."

('Where is Eva Peron?' 'Look for the name Duarte, over there'.) I could see this poor man slowly losing the will to live as his entire existence became reduced to an endless recitation of this solitary fact.

It was like 'Groundhog Day', except instead of living the same day over and over he was living the same 30 seconds. For all I know, his shift was due to last several hours.

By closing my eyes and *listening* to this scene, I could hear this man's slow descent into endless despair as he stood there, repeating himself, while nearby signs provided the same information. I used this as the basis for a TSS at the time (I was visiting the cemetery with a friend) and on other occasions during my visit to Buenos Aires. To this day, '"Buscá el apellido Duarte, por ahí," is the only thing I can say in Spanish. I don't get many opportunities to use it.

Want

There's often a gulf between what someone *is* doing and what they probably *want* or would prefer to do. I'm not saying you should unkindly or cruelly enjoy their misfortune. I'm just suggesting that, observed from a distance, this discrepancy can often provide the basis for a humorous TSS.

Here's another way to apply the 'want' cue. The world is full of notices forbidding things that you can't believe anyone would *want* to do in the first place!

Real-life example: I once had the pleasure of visiting Easter Island, one of the world's most enchanting destinations. It's a truly wonderful place, full of fascinating history, sights and monuments. While I was there, I saw a sign in a hotel telling people they couldn't stay in the coffee lounge all day. I found this rather baffling. Why would anyone *want* to? Who goes all the way to Easter Island just to *stay in the hotel* all day? I found myself imagining what their holiday photos look like. "Here's a nice view of the ceiling in the hotel reception area." This provided the path to a good TSS both while I was on Easter Island and when I got back to Chile.

It's also clear that people often *want* to do things that are remarkably stupid or dangerous. This is why we have signs in safari parks telling people *not* to get out of their car while passing near rhinos and tigers. Perhaps if anyone actually *wants* to do this, and regards it as a good idea, we should just let them. Having these people in the gene pool really isn't helping. The many things people want to do, or that other people *don't* want them to do, will often give you a path to a TSS. Human volition is a mystery.

Wear

If you're interested in the humorous version of the TSS, I suggest you become a fan of people-watching. In particular, notice the things people choose to wear. Of course, people have every right to wear whatever they want. Nonetheless, you'll often notice some rather odd, notable or unusual choices. I'm not saying you should approach the oddly dressed person and mock or tease them. However, when observing from a distance with a friend, you can often share a smile based on the curious ways some people choose to dress.

Real-life example. The other day I was enjoying a bit of people-watching with some friends. We saw a middle-aged man who clearly felt it was important to wear lots of colourful spots, dots and stripes. Everything he was wearing clashed conspicuously with everything else. Nothing matched. Why did he feel the need to dress like this? What's the story behind his curious sense of style? My friends and I enjoyed speculating about the reasons for this man's rather odd appearance. There really is no limit to the bewildering charm and strangeness of how people choose to present themselves to the world on a daily basis.

Words

Wherever you go, you're surrounded by words. Sometimes, people use words well, with clarity and elegance — for example, in books not written by me. However, you'll often see words mangled in notably unhelpful or confusing ways, such as signs that say the exact opposite of what they really mean. Officials who have to put up public notices seem to have a remarkable talent for creating confusion. Pay attention to words, and how poorly people use them, and you'll rarely be stuck for a humorous TSS.

Another thing you'll see, all over the world, are supposedly important signs you can't read. There are people in this world who put up important signs. There are also people who grow hedges and bushes. These two groups are locked in a grim, unyielding fight for supremacy. (See the DUCK for more.)

You can also get a good TSS from noticing words used *well* or in a pleasantly clever way. There are vast online galleries of funny and amusing signs that people have spotted. Keep your eyes open for examples of witty wording in your vicinity.

Practising The TSS

I've shared nine cue words or prompts that can provide a path to the humorous version of the TSS. These cues all overlap, as you may have noticed. For example, the 'Place' cue might involve a funny sign which could also be in the 'Words' category. You don't have to use all nine of these cues. If you prefer, just use one of the three sets I mentioned or choose the ones you find easiest to use. You can also make up your *own* cue words.

As with any other skill, regular practice is the only path to proficiency. How can you practise using the TSS and thinking of things to say? I have two suggestions.

Running The Cues

Here's an exercise I use when I'm teaching someone the TSS. We go out into the world and walk around for a minute or two until we reach a random spot. This could be indoors or outdoors, busy or quiet. We then go through the list of nine TSS cues and try to find something amusing to say based on each one of them. We consider how you might derive a TSS from 'Place', or 'Prop', or 'Problem'... and so on through the list.

This is a good workout for your mind. You can use it any time you want, whenever you have an opportunity to observe the world around you. Waiting for a bus? Look around, go through the list of TSS cues and see what you can come up with. Walking your dog through the park? Stop for a moment and try the cues again. Standing in line at the works canteen? Another opportunity to mentally run through the list of cues and see what occurs to you.

The Service Smile

An excellent way to develop TSS proficiency is to practise on all the wonderful people who work in the service industries. I'm referring to the people who serve you in stores, cafes and hotels and anyone else who performs a service role. I think highly of *all* these people and it's a shame they often don't get the thanks and appreciation they richly deserve. I suggest you take every opportunity to talk to them, show them some love and respect and... make them smile!

To repeat what I said before: never do this in a way that the person you're talking to will find annoying or inappropriate. For example, don't hold someone up if they are clearly busy and need to attend to a long line of people. Your aim is to cause one extra smile to appear in the world, not a weary and exasperated sigh.

Remember the notion of painless practice: use the TSS when it *doesn't* matter so you'll be good at it when it *does*. You can practise the TSS on all the wonderful people in the service industries. These conversations may not matter much. However, when an important conversation *does* come along, and you want to use the TSS, you'll have had lots of practice. The TSS is not a skill you can develop by thinking about it at home. You need to try using it in the real world.

The Girl On Malmö Station

If anyone ever doubts the *value* of the TSS, I tell them this story. I was once passing through the railway station in Malmö, Sweden. It was about 3pm. At one side of the concourse was a small stand selling tea, coffee and snacks. There was one young woman working there on her own. The stall wasn't busy and I was the only customer at the time.

I ordered my cup of tea. I then got talking to this woman behind the counter, starting with the ten-second smile. Her name was Karolyn and she had been there since 9am. I saw that she had been filling out a bit of paperwork, so I gave her a short personal reading based on her handwriting. (See Chapter 17, 'Cold reading', for details.)

I then said goodbye and was about to leave. Before I did, Karolyn thanked me *profusely* and was positively *beaming* with delight. She looked like she would have hugged me if she could. She explained, "I've been here since 9 o'clock this morning. You're the first person who has actually talked to me. I mean, really *talked*, like I'm a real person. Everyone else just gets their coffee and leaves. But you *talked* to me and gave me some time! It made a nice change. Thank you!!"

I've had similar experiences all over the world, with a wide range of service industry workers. Young and old, male and female... they all appreciate a touch of kindness. Talk to people. You never know when it might brighten someone's day. Also, if my experience is anything to go by, you'll get *lots* of free stuff and discounts without even asking! This isn't the reason to use the TSS but it is a nice incidental bonus.

Conversation As Play

The ten-second smile is part of a larger idea that's an important part of People Joy: conversation as play.

So long as you go about it the right way, that isn't tiresome or annoying, most people welcome the chance to smile, laugh and see life in a rather playful way. Of course, what is regarded as *acceptable* conversation, let alone *light-hearted* and *playful*, varies from one country, culture and set of social codes to the next. All I can say is that I've used the ten-second smile successfully in quite a few different countries so far, including Brazil, Finland, Romania, Jordan, Canada, Germany, Japan, Indonesia, Malaysia and Russia.

I sometimes wonder if social and cultural differences tend to get exaggerated. On the one hand, every country has its own social codes that we should respect. On the other hand, you can take the view that people are basically the same wherever you go. They enjoy sharing smiles and laughter because these are evolved signals of bonding and collective safety. I don't have any wisdom to offer on this subject or, for that matter, any other. I just think warm smiles and good connections make the world a better place for us all.

Playing is a great way to connect with other people. Life can be hard. People often have problems to deal with (and not all problems show up on the surface). If you brighten someone's day, in a way that they enjoy, I think this is a good thing to do.

Why Do This?

It would be trivially easy to misrepresent the ten-second smile and make it sound absurd. I am not suggesting you behave like an annoying idiot, desperate for attention, who constantly makes tiresome jokes. I am not suggesting you have to hide behind a 'mask' of humour because you're afraid to just be the real you and achieve authentic connections with people. The point is simply to set yourself the challenge of trying to elicit the smile or laughter reflex in a way that other people welcome and enjoy.

Why should you bother to do this? Because you appreciate the value of having active, intentional conversations rather than being stuck on autopilot. Because you're willing to try a little bit harder than offering stale, routine pleasantries. Because you're willing to be mentally alert and creative in the way you talk to people. Because you care enough about other people to make them smile and you know they are worth it. Because if people are smiling, they aren't hating or hurting. Because it's fun.

Being able to elicit the smile or laughter reflex whenever you want to is a wonderful skill to develop. You'll feel good *every single time* you use the TSS successfully. It's also a great way to share a bit of love. When people are smiling or laughing, they feel good. Be the person who creates a few smiles in the world today.

Chapter Summary

This chapter was all about one of my favourite People Joy techniques: the ten-second smile. I explained that this comes in two flavours: simple and humorous.

The main headings were:

- A transformative skill.

- Finding the fun: TSS cues.

- Practising the TSS.

- Conversation as play.

The three sets of cue words are:

Place / Prop / Problem
Sense / Similar / Sound
Want / Wear / Words

The next chapter is all about how you use your voice.

DUCK

Signs And Foliage

I mentioned the ongoing fight, which takes place all over the world, between people who put up important signs and notices and people who grow hedges and bushes. The available evidence suggests, sadly, that this grim and desperate conflict is unlikely to end within the foreseeable future.

I have more than just a passing interest in this struggle. In 2023 the United Nations convened a Peace Summit between the two factions. There were international delegations from SIGN (the Society for Instructive General Notices) and LEAF (the League Encouraging Advanced Foliage). I was there as an official observer. It gives me no pleasure to report that the whole thing descended into chaos. The UN had put up signs showing delegates how to reach the conference chamber. Unfortunately, someone — we'll never know who — had draped vines and other foliage in front of them so no one knew where to go. It was a complete fiasco.

I would happily share photos I've taken of this fight between signage and foliage if I had any. However, you won't be surprised to learn that I have no such photos to offer. I'd have to lead a pretty sad, empty life to have nothing better to do than go round my neighbourhood taking photos of signs obscured by bushes!

10. Voice Magic

"The human voice is the most beautiful instrument of all, but it is the most difficult to play."

— Richard Strauss

Progress Check

This is Part Three of People Joy, which consists of seven refinements to the material in Parts One and Two.

We just looked at the first of these refinements: the ten-second smile. Now let's take a look at an aspect of conversations that remarkably few people *ever* pay any attention to, even though it *clearly* makes a huge difference to your conversational success.

Part 1: Foundations

1. About Other People
2. About Yourself
3. About Conversations

Part 2: Talking

4. Before You Talk
5. When You Talk (1)
6. When You Talk (2)
7. When You Talk (3)
8. After You Talk

Part 3: Refinements

9. The Ten-second Smile
10. Voice Magic
11. More About Other People
12. More About You
13. The Joy Of Disagreement
14. Dealing With Anger

Part 4: Special Skills

15. The Art Of Selling
16. The Art Of Persuasion
17. The Art Of Cold Reading
18. Love Is What Works

An Amazing Device

Let me tell you about a device I can sell you.

This amazing device makes you more persuasive, more likeable and more likely to be listened to. It can help you to earn money and win respect. Think of almost anything you'd like to achieve and this device will at least double your chances of success.

Intrigued?

You might expect that any device that can do all of these things would be expensive. Well, think again... this device is actually *free!* What's more, you already own it but you (probably) just don't use it all that well. As you may have guessed from the title of this chapter, I'm referring to *your voice*.

Your Vocal Apparatus

Human vocal apparatus is fascinating, impressive and utterly unique in the animal kingdom. It's a shame that most of us barely even think about it, let alone appreciate its power and sophistication.

The story starts with your diaphragm, one of the largest muscles in your body. It sits just underneath your lungs. When your diaphragm contracts, you inhale air. When your diaphragm expands, this air gets pushed out of your lungs into a vertical tube called your trachea, also known as your windpipe.

This column of air passes through your larynx (voice box) which contains vocal cords, two small sets of layers of muscle that vibrate and produce the basic sound of your voice. This basic sound is modified by your tongue and lips to produce a range of sounds and effects that we learn to recognise as words. This is only a brief summary of how your voice works. I suggest you go online and spend a bit of time studying your vocal anatomy in order to appreciate how impressive it really is.

What does this have to do with People Joy? Everything! The more effectively you learn to use this amazing apparatus, the easier it becomes to achieve *all* of your People Joy goals. This leads me naturally on to the subject of vocalics.

Vocalics

Vocalics is the study of every aspect of how you use your voice *apart* from the actual words you say. Five elements of vocalics are:

Volume / **A**rticulation / **P**itch / **E**mphasis / **R**ate

These form the convenient acronym VAPER. Although these terms are fairly self-explanatory, let's take a look at them.

Volume. Your vocal apparatus can achieve an impressively wide range of subtly different effects, ranging all the way from the gentlest whisper to a roar that would scare off a lion. (Don't practise this in a library.) (Or try it with real lions.)

Taking it a step further, if you want you can learn the art of *vocal projection*. This is not the same as shouting. It's a much more controlled technique that adds intensity to your voice so it carries a long way. Most singers and performers learn how to do this.

Articulation. When you speak, you can use your lips to make every sound and syllable clear, separate and distinct. Alternatively, you can slur all your words together so they more or less merge into one sound. The more clearly your articulate, the easier it is for other people to follow what you're saying. However, if you take it too far, your speech begins to sound forced and unnatural.

Pitch. Everyone has their natural vocal range, from low notes to high. However, most people only use a small part of their range when they talk, which is a shame. The more of your range you use, within reason, the more interesting and listenable you tend to sound.

Emphasis. It's possible to talk in a monotonous way, giving every word the same emphasis as every other, so that nothing stands out and your speech is flat and grey. This makes you (a) harder to understand and (b) boring. Alternatively, you can speak using plenty of light and shade, colour and intonation, so that you emphasise some words or points more than others. This is much more engaging and pleasant to listen to.

Rate. You can speak slowly, so that every sentence takes forever. You can also speak quite rapidly, as if you're commenting on the final stage of a particularly exciting race.

Imagine that each of these five aspects of your voice is controlled by a dial with three settings: low, medium or high. You can try various permutations to see how they change your voice. For example:

Volume: low
Articulation: medium
Pitch: high
Emphasis: low
Rate: high

…or any other permutation you like. You have 243 permutations to play with. Once you start to experiment with your voice's potential and range, you'll soon see that your vocal apparatus is remarkably versatile (probably more so than you realised). You will start to appreciate that changing how you *use* your voice changes the *effect* it has. For example, you can change how listenable you are and how persuasive or authoritative you sound.

Teaching people about vocalics is one of my favourite things to do in a class or lecture situation because it involves some fun practical exercises. I'll describe them here so that you can try them yourself.

The Mismatch Exercise

This is a lot of fun!

Scene A. You're with someone you love with all your heart. The two of you are admiring some beautiful scenery. It's a quiet evening and the mood is tender and romantic. Think how you would say, "I love you with all my heart, and I always will."

Scene B. You're a military instructor training some new recruits. One of them doesn't seem to have much respect for your authority. Think how you would say, "When I say march, I expect you to *march*. Do you *understand?!*"

Scene C. You're a senior business executive who enjoys power and authority. You tend to express yourself in a rather icy and menacing way, like a stereotypical movie villain. You are facing someone from a different company whom you dislike. Think how you would say, "Your terms and conditions are unacceptable and, in my view, completely ridiculous."

Now, try swapping them around. Say the words from Scene A using the voice you would use for Scene B. Or say the words from Scene C using the voice you would use for Scene A. You will, of course, sound *ridiculous!* This is the whole point of the exercise. Deliberately mismatching voice and context like this is a powerful (and fun) way to illustrate two points:

- Your voice can produce many different effects.

- It's important to *match* how you use your voice to suit the context and your purpose.

There are many things you might want to achieve in a conversation: cheer up a friend, sell to a customer, ask someone out on a date, manage a team meeting, negotiate a difficult deal and so on. It *always* helps to use your voice to your best advantage.

How you use your voice always has an effect on the success of your conversations, whether you realise it or not. You may as well make sure the effect is a *positive* one. You want your voice to work *for* you rather than *against* you.

The Same Words Exercise

This exercise involves saying exactly the *same* words using *different* vocal styles to achieve different effects. Consider this short phrase:

"Hello. How are you?"

Try saying these words in a way that's appropriate to each of the following scenarios.

You are finally reunited with your romantic partner after quite some time apart.

You are a pompous, self-absorbed senior executive. You are meeting someone from the lower ranks whom you regard with disdain. You think meeting them is basically a waste of time.

You are one of life's endlessly bright, chirpy, cheerful characters. It's a busy Friday evening and you are welcoming someone to the pub where you work.

You are a cold, calculating villain meeting your greatest adversary. You have a cunning plan in mind that they don't know about. The fact that they don't know what you have in mind affords you some private amusement.

You unexpectedly run into someone you rather like. You're delighted to see them but also quite surprised.

This exercise, as well as being fun in a class situation, is another way to explore the impressive range of moods and effects your voice can produce. It helps you to realise that in every purposeful conversation, it's a good idea to modify your voice in a way that's likely to *serve your purpose*. If you want to sell, persuade or negotiate, the way you use your voice can significantly affect your success. If you want to enjoy social occasions and come across in a likeable way, the same is true — the way you use your voice can make a huge difference.

Volume Matters

I've mentioned that 'volume' is one of the five main elements of vocalics. Even if you ignore the rest of this chapter, please at least always try to use the appropriate *volume* when you're talking to people. Don't speak so softly that you leave the other person struggling to hear you. On the other hand, don't speak so loudly that you sound like you're addressing a rally in a stadium. Take the volume up or down so that the OP feels comfortable listening to you. This will greatly enhance your conversational success.

Invest In Some Coaching

If you want to learn more about how to use your voice successfully, consider investing in a couple of sessions with a professional vocal coach. It's true that *some* vocal coaches only work with singers. However, the majority are happy to work with *anyone* who wants to use their voice more successfully and effectively.

The vocal coach I personally recommend is my dear friend Marika Rauscher, an impressively talented singer who also provides vocal coaching and motivational talks. She's based in London but can work with clients anywhere. As well as being superb at what she does, she's also one of the most delightful people you could ever meet.

Chapter Summary

This chapter was about learning to make the most of your amazing vocal apparatus. The main headings were:

- An amazing device.

- Your vocal apparatus.

- Vocalics.

I mentioned five aspects of vocalics:

Volume / **A**rticulation / **P**itch / **E**mphasis / **R**ate

In the next chapter, we'll return to the subject of how you feel about other people.

DUCK

A Baden Baden Story

Knowing a little about how to use your voice can be useful in purely practical terms. I was once booked to present a talk and a magic show at a remarkable event called 'The Aristocrats Ball', held in the stunningly beautiful German town of Baden Baden. I had asked the organisers to provide a 'headset' microphone that would leave my hands free. Unfortunately, when I arrived I discovered that there had been an oversight. They didn't have a mic for me and there wasn't time to get one.

The organiser, looking distressed and apologetic, wasn't sure what to do. I reassured him and said I would simply use vocal projection instead. So I gave a talk and performed a show to 300 people, 'in the round' on a dance floor, without a microphone. I was able to do this because I've learned how to project my voice. Most of my friends who are performers and entertainers would have been able to do the same. We've all been through 'Oops! No microphone!' situations.

Incidentally, if you ever get a chance to visit Baden Baden, I suggest you take it. The town is extraordinarily beautiful with many 'picture perfect' views to enjoy.

The beautiful and picturesque spa town of Baden Baden.

Performing for 300 people without a mic!

11. More About Other People

"I believe there's nothing we can know
except that we should be kind to each other
and do what we can for people."

— Katharine Hepburn

Progress Check

Chapter 1 of this book, the first foundation chapter, was all about how you feel about other people.

In this chapter, I want to share a few more ideas regarding your attitude towards other people. These ideas are an important part of practising People Joy.

None Better Or Worse

For People Joy purposes, I suggest you adopt this attitude:

- You aren't better than anyone else.

- No one else is better than you.

At the risk of stating the obvious, you may be better (or worse) than someone else with regard to a *specific task*, such as playing the piano, leading a team, closing a sale, raising a child or driving a bus. What I'm recommending here is the view that you're no better or worse than anyone else in any *intrinsic, moral* or *absolute* sense. We're all clearly different from one another. However, 'different' doesn't mean 'better' or 'worse'.

Why is it a good idea, in People Joy terms, to adopt the view that you're no better than anyone else? Here are three reasons.

(1) If you believe you're better than other people, it detracts from your ability to find joy and fascination in them (as discussed in Chapter 1). You're unlikely to establish a good connection with someone you regard as inferior. Even if you attempt to disguise your feelings, some disdain will seep through your mask of acceptance. People rarely warm to a sneering attitude.

(2) The 'I'm better than you' attitude discourages collaboration, since people rarely want to work with someone who looks down on them. Collaboration is one of life's joys and part of every success story. You want more collaboration in your life, not less.

(3) Feelings of superiority have toxic side effects. Imagine a situation where one person feels superior to someone else. Little by little, the corrosion spreads and becomes tribal. Now you have one group in society feeling superior to another group and blaming them for most of society's problems. The toxicity gradually spreads and intensifies. This leads to a large tribe, or an entire race or nation, feeling superior to another. History tells us how tragically this can end. The story of 'I'm better than you' seldom has a happy ending. It leads to division, distrust, hate and, eventually, violence or war. We don't have to go down this path. I'm no historian, but I'm fairly sure there has never been a war between nations who see each other as different but nonetheless cool and interesting.

Why adopt the attitude of 'No one else is better than me'? Again, let me offer three reasons.

(1) If you think anyone's better than you, in the absolute sense, it undermines your self-greatness so your light shines a little less brightly. This isn't a good thing to do to yourself and it deprives others of your light and brilliance. It's all right to recognise that other people are better than you at specific tasks. The point is that this doesn't affect your worth and value as a person.

(2) 'They're better than me' is a case of 'conparing', which we looked at in Chapter 2. The opportunity to compare yourself to someone else isn't one you have to take and is completely pointless.

(3) Putting yourself down fosters the 'I'm not good enough / they wouldn't be interested in me' mentality. This type of negative self-talk stops you from approaching people, reaching out to them or even asking them out on a date! It's possible that the other person would *love* to meet you and vice versa. You don't know until you know. Don't discard these possibilities before you've even explored them.

You may or may not *actually* believe that no one's better than anyone else in the intrinsic or absolute sense. Nonetheless, I suggest that *for People Joy purposes* this is the best attitude to adopt. If you don't believe it's true, adopt it anyway when you talk to people. You might lose one or two points for integrity but, on the plus side, you'll get all the benefits and rewards of talking to people with kindness, respect, appreciation and understanding.

Expect, Accept, Respect

This chapter, an extension of Chapter 1, is about your attitude towards other people and what tends to work best in People Joy terms. Moving on from 'all different, none better or worse', I'd like to propose another principle: don't try to fight human nature. *Expect* people to be the way they are (with good points and bad, riches and glitches), *accept* them as they are and give them your *respect*.

As you may have noticed, people can be careless, unreliable, clumsy, forgetful and unfair. The list of human flaws and failings is not a short one. Given that this is the case, you can either spend your life fighting *against* human nature or trying to work *with* it.

The first choice involves constantly moaning about other people and their abundant flaws while wishing, with an exasperated and rather self-righteous sigh, that they'd just try a bit harder. It also involves frequently feeling angry, annoyed, dismayed and let down. You may also develop a rather dismissive attitude towards people in general and start to deplore the fact that you seem to be the only reliable person left in the world. This can be rather a lonely position in which to find yourself.

If you try to fight against human nature, you will fail. People aren't going to change even if they have your shiny, radiant example of perfection to follow. In addition, you'll add to the stress in your life, struggle to make good connections with people and acquire a reputation for being prickly and bad-tempered. You'll find your path through life rather tough because people come to think of you as 'the difficult one'.

Instead of trying to work against human nature, or fix it, I suggest you choose to work *with* it. This option is more realistic and involves a lot less stress and frustration. You'll find it much easier to attract friends and get their help and support. This, in turn, will make it easier to achieve whatever type of success you want for yourself.

Expect. Accept. Respect. (Don't reject.)

When People Let You Down

One part of 'Expect, Accept, Respect' can be very challenging: how to react when people let you down. This is certainly going to happen from time to time. If you want to practise People Joy, and enjoy all the benefits, you need to give some thought as to how you deal with these difficult situations.

For illustration purposes, let's say you work in an office. Mike, from the company's *other* office, was meant to deliver some documents you need for an important meeting that starts in fifteen minutes. He has failed to do so. You call him, rather frantically, and it turns out he's still in the other office, having completely forgotten all about this. It's now too late to get the documents to you which leaves you with a tricky problem to deal with.

You now have two options.

SCAT

Option (1) is the 'Fighting Against Human Nature' option. You start by feeling superior to Mike because *you*, of course, would never be so unreliable. You give yourself the cheap ego stroke of being the radiant beacon of excellence that you imagine yourself to be.

Next, you experience a stress reaction, get angry and indulge in a temper tantrum. This might feel temporarily satisfying but looks childish to anyone watching. You poison yourself and the atmosphere in the office with ugly stress hormones. You say abusive things about Mike: "What a useless idiot!" When people tell Mike what you said, which they will, he won't like it. From that point on, he'll prefer to have as little as possible to do with you, which could be your loss. His knowledge and experience might one day have been useful.

None of these steps help the situation but they do take up time and now the meeting is just ten minutes away. This is the **SCAT** option. It stands for Stressed, Cranky, Abusive Tantrum.

HEAL

Option (2) is the 'Work With Human Nature' option. Your starting point is to be aware of three things.

You are aware that you can't change human nature any more than you can make rain fall upwards. This being the case, you don't waste your time trying. You would just exhaust yourself and look silly.

You are aware that today isn't the only day. On this occasion, Mike made a mistake. On another day, *you* might let *him* down. Or Mike might be the super helpful star who saves the day.

You are also aware that nobody ever *intends* to do something wrong or make a mistake. It's not as if this is anyone's preferred plan for the day. Also, it's difficult to blame Mike for occasionally being forgetful given that he never chose the factors that shaped who he is (a point which I'll elaborate on in the next section). Your goal, in People Joy terms, is to develop the best relationship you can with Mike. Not with a shiny, flawless version of Mike but with Mike as he is.

Next, you update your mental model of the world you live in. An unfortunate thing has happened and you can't make it un-happen.

You give a shrug and say to yourself or to anyone else present, "Well, people do sometimes forget things. We've all done it. I'm sure Mike didn't *mean* to. He's normally quite reliable. Maybe he's just got a lot on at the moment." You don't introduce anger, abuse or a tantrum into the situation. Everything stays harmonious.

Then you go into problem-solving mode. I described one way to do this in Chapter 3. A problem has come up but you're not going to scare yourself with the fear of not being able to handle it. You remind yourself that you're pretty darned good at solving problems. Here's a chance to show off your problem-solving super powers! Maybe you can run the meeting without the documents. Maybe there's a creative workaround. Maybe you can postpone the meeting or go ahead but keep it short and follow up later.

This is the **HEAL** option. It stands for Harmonious, Empathic, Accepting and Leads to problem-solving. For People Joy purposes, I recommend you take the HEAL option. It gets easier with practice.

When you react in this way, you stay free from stress. This is a really good move in terms of looking after your health and the health of the office environment. You don't look silly to everyone else and you don't make an enemy. You get a reputation for being able to get along with people and for handling problems in a mature and productive way. You don't get the 'I'm more reliable than everyone else' ego stroke, which is entirely based on your private delusion of superiority. You do get the 'I manged that situation very well' ego stroke, which is based in reality.

It's also worth remembering that hubris is a thing. Today, you might enjoy ranting about how superior and efficient you are, especially compared to that 'idiot' Mike. However, I promise there will come a day when *you* make a glorious mess of something and everyone will take great delight in your downfall. They'll savour the sight of your conspicuous failure and think, "Who's the idiot now, eh?!" There's no need to ever put yourself in this position. As Shakespeare has it:

> *"Tempt not the squalid snare of Fate's embrace*
> *With declaration loud of virtue's haul*
> *For then shall folly's shame reshape thy face*
> *And craft delighted witness of thy fall."*
> (Titus Andronicus, Act III, scene ii)

Your 'BEST MASK' Story

Before ending this chapter, I feel it might be useful to revisit the point about whether anyone is better or worse than anyone else in the moral or absolute sense.

This question takes us into the complex area of philosophy called 'Free Will Versus Determinism'. If you're interested in this subject, I highly recommend two books: 'The Tyranny Of Merit' by Michael J. Sandel and 'Determined' by Robert Sapolsky. These superb books have made a big difference to my own opinions about whether it makes sense to regard one person as 'better' than another.

In any discussion about comparative merit or worth, the starting point is to ask how people turn out to be the way they are. Here's a simple way of looking at it. Everyone on the planet is largely the product of eight 'BEST MASK' factors:

Background. Their genes, where they were born and how their parents raised them.

Education / Experience. This covers the extent of their access to education, which may have involved bias or indoctrination, plus whatever they've learned from life, media and culture.

Skills. The things they've learned to do well.

Talents and aptitudes. The things they are innately good or bad at, as determined by their body and their brain chemistry.

Motives. Their set of feelings, emotions, drives and proclivities.

Awareness. The extent of their picture of the world and their role within it. (Someone may not realise they live in an invisible bubble of privilege if they're never made aware of it.)

Struggles. The problems, insecurities or innate difficulties they have to contend with, such as being prone to depression or trauma-based anxiety.

Knowledge. All the facts, figures and thoughts they carry around in their head — some of which may, of course, be warped, biased or mistaken.

These eight factors are largely a matter of pure luck. You didn't choose your genes, geography or genius. You didn't choose whether you got a good education, a bad one or no education at all. You didn't choose how prone you are to depression or learning difficulties.

Once someone has come into this life, shaped by their BEST MASK factors, they are a walking collage of randomly allocated strengths, weaknesses, talents and inclinations. They spend their days trying to move towards what feels good and away from what feels bad. This isn't always easy and life doesn't come with a guarantee of fairness. People just do the best they can with what they've got, making trips round the Sun in search of the fun.

For this reason, I don't regard anyone as better than anyone else in a moral or intrinsic sense. I see everyone as the work-in-progress collage of their BEST MASK ingredients.

The Bird And The Fish

Here's another way to think about comparative merit. In a contest between a bird and a fish, which of them will win? Obviously, if the challenge is to reach the top of a tree then the bird will win. On the other hand, if it's about swimming under water to reach the bottom of a lake, it's very likely that the fish will enjoy a significant victory.

You can say that one is better than the other at a specific task, such as flying or breathing under water. However, it doesn't make sense to say one is 'better' in an absolute sense. The bird didn't choose to be born with wings. The fish didn't choose to be born with gills. You wouldn't blame the bird for not being good at swimming under water. You wouldn't blame the fish for it's inability to reach the top of a tree.

I feel the same way about people. Your BEST MASK factors shaped your body, the physical nature of your brain and your brain chemistry. As a result, you have more natural aptitude for some *types* of tasks than others. For example, you might have impressive practical skills but little taste for academic study — or vice versa. This is why I believe that we're all different but no one is better or worse than anyone else in an absolute sense.

A Complicated Subject

Some people strongly oppose the idea that no one is better or worse than anyone else. They contend that it undermines the whole notion of free will, morality and personal accountability. After all (they say), if the thief had no choice but to turn out the way he did, on what basis should we hold him to account and punish him?

I'm not intellectually strong and have never claimed to be. It's perfectly possible that I'm wrong about 'all different, none better' and the deterministic outlook. I've been wrong about many things in my life and I know that just because I've read a few books doesn't mean I'm right. All I can say is that the subjects of free will and comparative merit are nuanced and complicated. In 'Determined', Sapolsky explores the issue of moral values and accountability in tremendous depth and detail. If you're interested in this subject, I suggest you read what he has to say or at least watch some of his videos and interviews on YouTube. He's a fascinating character and argues his case very cogently.

Chapter Summary

You can think of this chapter as an extension to Chapter 1. It offered a few additional ideas regarding how you think and feel about other people. The main headings were:

- None better or worse.

- Expect, accept, respect.

- When people let you down.

- Your 'BEST MASK' story.

The next chapter is all about the joy of disagreement. "No, it isn't!" "Yes it is!"

DUCK

The Joy Of Collaboration

In this chapter, I said it's a bad move to do anything that makes other people less inclined to collaborate with you.

Life has taught me to *love* the notion of collaboration. When different people combine their respective strengths and talents, wonderful things can happen. I'm sure you have your own favourite examples. It took thousands of people, all contributing their various areas of expertise, to land a man on the moon back in 1969. Every architectural triumph is the product of many minds and hands. Collaboration is part of *every* successful business and, of course, lies at the core of love, romance and relationships. It's often said that it takes a village to raise a child.

I experience the joy of collaboration on a regular basis. Self-employed people tend to help one other all the time. This is also true of the PACE community (Performers, Artists, Creatives, Entertainers) where calls for help rarely go unanswered. Collaboration is one way in which real magic comes into the world and makes a tangible difference. I suggest you cultivate *more* opportunities in your life for collaboration to flourish rather than *fewer*.

An Apology

It took me a long time to learn to respond to being let down the HEAL way. There were countless times in my life when I took the SCAT option instead. In my case, it wasn't so much a case of getting angry as rather publicly having a moan about other people failing to be quite as perfectly reliable as myself. I'd like to apologise to anyone who had the misfortune to be in the vicinity whenever I reacted in this way. We live, we learn, we watch the world turn.

12. More About You

"True happiness arises, in the first place,
from the enjoyment of one's self, and in the
next, from the friendship and conversation
of a few select companions."

— Joseph Addison

Progress Check

This is the second of the seven sections in Part Three.

Chapter 2 of this book, the second foundation chapter, dealt with how you feel about yourself. In this chapter, I want to return to this subject and offer a few more ideas about you, your life and putting People Joy into practice.

Part 1: Foundations

1. About Other People
2. About Yourself
3. About Conversations

Part 2: Talking

4. Before You Talk
5. When You Talk (1)
6. When You Talk (2)
7. When You Talk (3)
8. After You Talk

Part 3: Refinements

9. The Ten-second Smile
10. Voice Magic
11. More About Other People
12. More About You
13. The Joy Of Disagreement
14. Dealing With Anger

Part 4: Special Skills

15. The Art Of Selling
16. I Doubt Anyone Is
17. Reading These By Now
18. Love Is What Works

The Moth Principle

Many people have this attitude: 'I'll feel happy and positive when I get what I want'.

Here's a better alternative: 'I'll get what I want when I feel happy and positive'.

I hasten to add that this has nothing to do with mysticism or wishful thinking. It's an entirely pragmatic way of understanding how life works. Let me explain what I mean.

In the Introduction, I said the single most important factor in achieving success is always the same: **other people**. More specifically, how well you connect and communicate with them. This being the case, it's worth remembering that people are like moths: they feel drawn towards the light. When people can sense love, warmth, joy and positive energy in you, they feel drawn to you. (When people sense doom and gloom in you, they're less likely to want to connect *even if* they're sympathetic and understanding.)

When people feel drawn to you, they're more likely to want to help you or to work with you. Since every person is a door to countless opportunities, it follows that the more people who are drawn to you, the easier your path will be. You're more likely to come across the right opportunities you need to achieve your goals.

Light attracts people. People bring opportunities. Opportunities are your path to the success you want. This is how life works.

For this reason, when you talk to people, it pays to emphasise the positive aspects of your life and give out as much good energy as you can. I'm not saying you should lie or pretend everything is wonderful when it isn't. You can be honest about your life and feelings. The point is that it's in your interests to give out as much positive energy as you can. You can *honestly acknowledge* your negative feelings while also preferring to *focus on*, and *talk about*, the positive ones.

This doesn't only apply to the way you talk to people. It applies to every way in which you publicly express yourself, such as social media posts. Give out as much positive energy as you can. Try to spread light rather than darkness.

If your positive energy is running a bit low, which can happen now and again, there's an easy fix: practise the art of practical kindness. Every time you're kind to someone, even if that person happens to be a complete stranger, you feel better about yourself and re-charge your positive energy.

Let someone get on the bus before you (even if you were actually there first). Help someone who's struggling to carry a heavy suitcase. Offer to do some free babysitting so your friend and their partner can have a night out. Give up your seat to someone who might need it more than you. Hold the door open for the next person. If you're tall, help someone to reach the top shelf in the supermarket. Clear the snow from your neighbour's drive as well as your own. Help a young mother get the pram off the bus. When someone new joins the team, office or neighbourhood, be the one who makes them feel welcome and helps them to settle in.

You can also practise practical kindness online. Go on social media, see what your friends are up to and post a few comments that are kind, helpful or supportive. They've had bad news? Commiserate. They've had good news? Congratulate. They'd like some help or feedback? Cooperate.

When you only focus on yourself, you can only connect with yourself. This is like a battery trying to be its own source of fuel. It doesn't work. When you practise some love and kindness, and focus *outside* of yourself, you can connect with other people. This connection is how you recharge the light inside yourself.

Kindness fuels the light inside you. Light attracts people. People bring opportunities. Opportunities are your path to the success you want. This is how life works. You only have to remember five words.

Kindness > **Li**ght > **P**eople > **O**pportunities > **S**uccess

KLiPOS.

It's that simple. If you like, I can wrap this up in a few hundred pages of verbiage that might, if you're in a generous mood, look vaguely like ancient wisdom. I'm also willing, if you want, to make up a story and say I meditated on top of a mountain for a year, communing with the cosmos, to discover The Way Of The Badger or something like that. However, I prefer to keep it simple.

MEDS LAKE

Here are a few good ideas related to The Moth Principle. They're only suggestions so feel free to ignore them.

The term 'MEDS LAKE' is simply a way to remember eight points. Every day, try to take good care of your MEDS:

- Meditation.

- Exercise.

- Diet.

- Sleep.

These are four important elements of good mental, emotional and physical health. It's also a good idea, if you can, to try to make sure every day features some LAKE:

- Learning.

- Awareness.

- Kindness.

- Enjoyment / fun.

The *more* you take care of your MEDS LAKE, the *more* likely you are to be someone that people like and are drawn to. The *less* you take care of your MEDS LAKE, the *less* likely this is to be the case. Here are some brief notes about these eight ideas.

Meditation

There are many different ways to meditate. You can find out all about them, and find the best one for you, by going to a class, asking friends, watching YouTube videos or using other online resources. There's no question that regular meditation benefits your mental and emotional health. I'm very glad that I learned how to meditate many years ago. There are no downsides, it doesn't have to take up much time and it's completely free.

Exercise

Cardiovascular fitness is the single greatest gift you can give to yourself. It makes every aspect of your life better and there are no downsides Also, depending on how you go about getting fit, it's basically free. You don't *have* to join a gym. You could just go jogging three times a week and stick at it until you can comfortably manage five kilometres (three miles). It's amazing what a difference physical fitness makes to your life.

Diet

Some things you can eat and drink tend to lead to, and support, good health. Some will lead you in the opposite direction, perhaps towards obesity and related problems. You don't need a lecture on nutrition and food groups to appreciate the difference. You know that fresh fruit and veg are more likely to lead to good health than junk food, sugar and beer. Of course, it's up to you how you want to live your life. However, perhaps you could try loving yourself enough to make some good choices. Health feels good.

Sleep

Every expert in the world will tell you that getting enough sleep is essential for good health. It's not just a question of how *much* sleep you get. It's also about getting good *quality* sleep, so you enjoy all the mental and physical benefits. To be at your best, get plenty of rest. If you'd like to find out a bit more, I suggest you read Matthew Walker's justly popular and widely admired book, 'Why We Sleep'.

Learning

It's a good idea to try to learn something every day, so you go to bed knowing more than you did when you woke up. Read (or listen to) some non-fiction books on subjects that interest you. Look at articles and videos online that expand your knowledge or teach you new skills. Learn from library books, from experience and from friends. Learn by playing and experimenting. Learn a new language or a musical instrument. Learning is fulfilling, rewarding and (depending on how you go about it) *mostly* free.

Awareness

I don't know about you and your life. You may be dealing with all sorts of problems. Even so, try to stay *aware* and *mindful* of what's good about your life. It may help to think about things you have that (a) many people in history didn't have, and (b) many people in the world still don't have.

If you have access to clean drinking water whenever you want it, this is excellent news. Many people in history didn't have this luxury and had to go a long way to get drinkable water. Many people in the world still don't have this.

If you are currently living in a *mostly* civilised and peaceful part of the world, and don't have to deal with the horrors of war every day, you're doing well. If you don't suffer from the types of bigotry and prejudice that many people have to contend with, be glad of it. Try to be aware of any invisible bubbles of privilege you enjoy. All in all, try to remain aware and mindful of whatever's good about your life, even if you have your troubles and problems.

Kindness

I talked about this in 'The Moth Principle'. Try to perform acts of practical kindness every day. There are always opportunities to do this if you look for them.

When you're kind to other people, you body produces a hormone called oxytocin (associated with the experience of love, contact and kindness). It also produces dopamine (associated with completing tasks, self-care and occasional bits of indulgence). These are both what might be called 'feel good' hormones. You can fill yourself up with them as much as you like and they're free.

Enjoyment / Fun

Try to build some enjoyment and fun into every day of your life. Spend some time doing the things that you like and that give you pleasure, even if they're silly and trivial. Leisure time is important. Even grown-ups need some play time and it promotes mental and emotional health. Some fun every day keeps the doctor away.

Freedom From Stress

In Chapter 3, I talked about being a Freedom Hero and living your life free from self-doubt, fear and conflict. I'd like to suggest adding one more freedom to the list: freedom from stress.

The relevance to People Joy should be fairly clear. People like people who don't seem anxious, nervous and stressed out all the time. A sense of calm has lasting charm. Also, the better you are at reducing stress in your own life, the more you can help others to reduce it in theirs. We all prefer the skiing instructor *without* the broken leg.

A good first step towards a stress-free life is to do a little reading and find out more about the subject. The more you understand about a problem, the easier it is to deal with. Wikipedia is one good starting place. It offers an excellent article on stress together with several links for further reading.

As for actually freeing yourself from stress, the best move is to give yourself the gift of cardiovascular fitness. There are several ways to get fit and some are basically free, such as regular jogging. The fitter you are, the less of a problem stress becomes. When fitness goes up, stress goes down.

Getting enough sleep and learning how to meditate can also help to alleviate stress. Of course, if stress is what's *preventing* you from sleeping, this advice might sound rather hollow.

What else? I think it helps to be aware that you can respond to anxious situations in two ways: *emotionally* or *methodically*. As I mentioned in Chapter 3, they're both good options in different ways. It's perfectly all right to respond to situations emotionally *if* you can do so safely and you need the release. The alternative is to respond methodically, which means calmly going into problem-solving mode. Which square are you on? Which square do you want to get to? What are the available options and what are the pros and cons of each one? From your analysis, which seems to be the *best* option?

Another good way to achieve freedom from stress is to get help from a qualified therapist or counsellor. There's no shame in seeking help of this type. Stress is seriously bad news that can lead to all sorts of problems. It's worth taking whatever steps you need to achieve and enjoy a stress-free life.

Self-belief

If you want to practise People Joy, always believe in yourself. You might feel this is largely the same as being free from self-doubt (which we've already covered). While there is some overlap, I see them as two slightly different qualities. Being free from self-doubt is about escaping negative feelings. Believing in yourself is about embracing positive feelings. More specifically, it's about your self-greatness: finding happiness in who you are, your capabilities, your potential and what you can bring into the world.

A vital part of believing in yourself is *to also believe in other people*. These two ideas go together. Believing in yourself and your potential involves believing in other people as well. This may sound strange at first but it isn't really. Your success will always involve getting assistance or cooperation from other people. It therefore helps to regard other people as capable of getting things done. In addition, believing in other people creates a positive mood and a bit of golden light that reflects back at you.

The TAL Principle

As part of believing in yourself, I recommend you embrace the TAL Principle. 'TAL' in this case stands for 'Talking And Listening'. From time to time, say to yourself:

- I am worth talking to.

- I am worth listening to.

You might find it useful to write out three reasons why you're worth talking to and another three reasons why you're worth listening to. For example: 'I am worth talking to because I'm a really good listener / people tell me they like my advice / I can often see connections that other people perhaps can't see.'

'I am worth listening to because I usually have a fun story or two to share / I'm passionate about my work and people say they like my energy / I'm told I'm good at putting things into perspective.'

If you want People Joy in your life, remember that you're worth talking to and worth listening to (and so is everyone else).

Vision

People tend to respond positively to people who have a clear vision about their life and their path. Get to the point where you know where you're going with your life and you have clear plans for the future, both short-term and long-term. Your plans, direction and focus constitute your vision. The clearer it is, the better.

Always be happy to tell people about your plans *if* the subject happens to come up in conversation. I don't suggest you meet someone and immediately start droning on about your glorious plans and intentions. However, if someone *asks* you about your plans, it's good to be able to outline what you intend to achieve, how and when.

Incidentally, if you're in charge of a team or department, it's an important part of good leadership to have a clear vision that people can follow and support. People can't feel loyal to a vague, fuzzy plan. They can't feel inspired by it either. Clarity is your friend. When you *explain* your vision, try to do so using three clear points, each short enough for people to remember. A good formula to use is 'keyword + phrase', like this:

Range. Expand our product range based on customer feedback.

Assembly. Trim delivery times by bringing final assembly back in-house.

Orders. Make online ordering easier and simpler.

Want to make this even better? Organise your three points so the first letters of your three keywords form a word or acronym. In this example, you could rearrange them so the first letters spell 'ORA' (Orders / Range / Assembly.) This makes it easy for anyone to understand and remember your vision for the team. All they have to remember is 'ORA' and the three keywords.

Even if you don't really feel you need to make three points, try to find three things to say anyway. Why? Because it's psychologically comfortable and memorable. The so-called 'rule of three' crops up in many different fields, from rhetoric and persuasive public-speaking to writing comedy scripts.

The Rational Path

Here's my final suggestion for this chapter.

People are not, and never will be, mostly rational creatures. For most people, most of the time, rationality isn't very high on the agenda. People can *try* to be rational and analytical when the need arises, such as when trying to work out how the timer works on the new cooker. However, they mostly experience life through their feelings and emotions. This isn't going to change. If you want to drive yourself mad with frustration, go through life expecting people to be rational, consistent and logical. Your expectations will be cruelly shattered on a routine basis.

With all that said, I think it's a good idea to be a *mostly* rational person, especially when you're wondering what's real and true (as opposed to lies, myths and the photographs in recipe books). It's really useful, as you make your way through life, to understand the difference between good and bad reasoning. To this end, I suggest you go online and look at lists of common logical fallacies and how to avoid them. It's well worth knowing about fallacies such as 'Straw Man', 'No True Scotsman', 'Survivorship Bias' and 'Post hoc ergo propter hoc'. Being able to spot bad reasoning when people try to use it on you is a great asset in life. It means you don't get conned and misled quite so often.

Another good idea is to understand what 'the scientific method' really means. It refers to a *process* of observation, hypothesis, experiment, data and peer review. How this process was developed, and why it works so successfully (albeit never perfectly), is a fascinating subject to read about.

I believe rationality is a good way to either gain or preserve your intellectual freedom. Yes, there should be room in life for passion, feelings, art, fun and those parts of the human spirit that lie beyond cold, hard facts. However, when you're trying to work out what's real and true, I believe that a rational outlook helps a lot. In fact, I'd say it helps more than anything else.

You may or may not agree with me about this. If you don't, then let's enjoy the warm, golden glow of peaceful disagreement. If we ever meet, perhaps I'll learn something from you — in which case you will have done me a favour.

Chapter Summary

This chapter discussed various aspects of how you feel about yourself, and choose to live your life, that relate to People Joy. You can see it as an extension of Chapter 1. The main headings were:

- The Moth Principle.

- MEDS LAKE.

- Freedom from stress.

- Self-belief.

- Vision.

- The rational path.

MEDS LAKE is a way to remember eight subjects:

Meditation / Exercise / Diet / Sleep
Learning / Awareness / Kindness / Enjoyment

DUCK

Learning

In this chapter, I mentioned it's a good idea to learn a foreign language or a musical instrument. With regard to learning a language, I'm afraid I'm unable to set a good example. It's one of the many things my brain simply refuses to do. As soon as someone starts trying to tell me that nouns have a gender, my brain refuses to go any further along the path.

However, I *have* successfully taught myself to play the guitar. I was inspired to do so by one of the moments that changed my life. When I was 15, I heard Mike Oldfield's hauntingly beautiful and seductive album, 'Ommadawn'. From that point on, I felt compelled to learn how to play the guitar. This was long before the internet era and I had no teacher, no lessons, no books. I just had to work it out for myself — a slow process which now, forty years later, is still in progress.

Am I a good guitarist? No. In fact, I'm quite a bad one. I'd say I'm about as bad as it's possible to be after forty years of almost daily practice. Nonetheless, playing the guitar has given me countless hours of pleasure throughout my life. I think learning to play a musical instrument, even if you never reach a high standard, is hugely rewarding. It's also a remarkably effective way to deal with stress or anxiety. When you play a musical instrument, it feels as if you shut down one set of mental circuits and switch on a different set. This can help you to calm down and to settle anxious thoughts. At least, that's how it works for me.

Leading

I touched on the subject of leadership and being able to share your 'vision' with your team. If you're interested in this area, there's a brilliant short poem by Roger McGough you should read. It's called 'The Leader'. It's only eight lines long yet it makes an excellent point about leadership in a beautifully elegant way. I can't reproduce it here because it's copyright but you can find it online if you want to. The first line is, "I wanna be the leader." I think you'll like it.

Rationality Notes

In the 'Rationality' section, I made the point that human beings tend not to be very rational. In fact, people are capable of believing more or less anything — even things that are absurd or utterly nonsensical. This point was gloriously illuminated by Charles Mackay's famous book, 'Extraordinary Popular Delusions and the Madness of Crowds', first published in 1841. I expect most of my readers will know about this book but I'm mentioning it for the few who don't. It's a truly astounding work and well worth reading. I'm aware that there are some modern equivalents, such as 'More Extraordinary Popular Delusions' by Joseph Bulgatz although, alas, I haven't so far read any of them.

While we're talking about rationality, I'd also like to mention Arthur Koestler's book, 'Janus: A Summing Up', in which he puts forward a theory as to *why* people aren't very rational. His argument, in very simple terms, is that the different parts of the human brain, having evolved at different times, are 'wired up' in a rather arbitrary and unhelpful way that leads to what one might describe as 'mixed signals'. It's as if the primitive 'lizard brain' parts and the cerebral cortex get in one another's way, so emotions sometimes derail one's rational faculties. I thought I'd mention this in case any of you want to read the book for yourselves.

If you're interested in the difference between good and bad reasoning, I *strongly* recommend that you look up something called 'The Wason Selection Task', also known as 'The Four-Card Problem'. If you share this reasoning test with a class or group, only about 10% are likely to come up with the right answer! In my experience, even when you give people the correct answer they often struggle to understand *why* it's the right answer. This leads to some interesting discussions.

13. The Joy Of Disagreement

"Si je diffère de toi, loin de te léser, je t'augmente"

— *Antoine de Saint Exupéry*

(If I differ from you, far from harming you, I increase you.)

Progress Check

I'm going to conclude Part Three by discussing two subjects that often come up whenever I talk about *People Joy*. The first is how to handle disagreement and the second is how to manage anger — either someone else's or your own.

Part 1: Foundations

1. About Other People
2. About Yourself
3. About Conversations

Part 2: Talking

4. Before You Talk
5. When You Talk (1)
6. When You Talk (2)
7. When You Talk (3)
8. After You Talk

Part 3: Refinements

9. The Ten-second Smile
10. Voice Magic
11. More About Other People
12. More About You
13. The Joy Of Disagreement
14. Dealing With Anger

Part 4: Special Skills

15. The Art Of Selling
16. The Art Of Persuasion
17. The Art Of Cold Reading
18. Love Is What Works

Belief Formation: Life Through A Lens

As you may have noticed, there's a lot of disagreement in the world. (Feel free to be impressively witty at this point and say, "No there isn't!") Disagreement itself is never a problem. The way some people *react* to disagreement can be a problem. Sadly, disagreement can lead to anger, aggression and fights. On a small scale it can lead to people falling out and deciding to dislike one another. On a large scale it can lead to hate, violence and war.

If you want to practise People Joy, with all the benefits it brings into your life, you need to know how to handle disagreement. The first step is to understand how people arrive at their views and beliefs.

A Brief Account Of Lens Formation

A baby is born. Let's call him John. As he grows up, John slowly pieces together a view of how the world works and what he regards as 'reality'. Many factors will influence what John believes. I listed some of these in Chapter 11 using the acronym 'BEST MASK'. These factors include where in the world John was born, how his parents raised him, his access to education... and so on. Most of these influential factors are matters of random chance.

As John matures into adulthood, he arrives at a view of what's real or unreal, true or false, based on all of his formative influences. This is sometimes referred to as John's 'lens' — the set of beliefs that define his perception and understanding of the world.

This lens is always self-serving to some extent. Most people develop a lens that favours their own interests and casts them in the happy role of being in the right tribe, with the right ideas, most of the time.

It's true that people's beliefs can evolve and mature as they reach adulthood. What John believes when he's thirty might be notably different from what his parents taught him as a youngster. However, even this process is largely governed by factors that lie outside of John's control, such as his *opportunities* to outgrow his formative influences, his *inclination* to do so and whether he has the *mental flexibility* to adopt new ideas. In the vast majority of cases, a person's beliefs owe a great deal to a set of random factors (BEST MASK) they didn't choose.

Preserving The Lens: Confirmation Bias

In John's mature adult life, there will be two sets of influences that continue to shape his beliefs: the ones he actively seeks and the ones that he doesn't.

The first set consists of all the newspapers, magazines and books that John chooses to read, the TV shows and videos he chooses to watch, whichever sources of news he follows, the people he chooses to associate with and so on. Most people choose sources that either support, or are at least compatible with, their existing lens. For example, if you have developed a strong political or religious view, you will tend to associate on a regular basis with other people who share that view.

The influences that John does *not* actively go looking for include all the social and cultural 'noise' that surrounds him every single day of his life. While he can try to filter it to some extent, there will always be a large number of sources that he's exposed to regardless of his personal choices.

If John comes across anything that *supports* his lens, or is at least *compatible* with it, he tends to accept this as being real and true. In most cases, he does this automatically and without thinking about it. The new 'information' gets mentally tucked away as part of John's lens. It becomes another piece of evidence that his understanding of how the world works happens to be true and correct.

If John encounters anything that *contradicts* his lens, he tends to either ignore it or discredit it. There are countless ways to do this. Here are four examples:

- Everyone knows that's not true. It's just people talking nonsense and making up whatever suits them.

- That source is biased, unfair or inaccurate. It's just recycled propaganda that we've heard before.

- That 'information' is out of date or isn't comprehensive or ignores some relevant factors.

- The people who say that are also the people who say this [mention a stupid or horrible thing they also say].

Even if people are faced with compelling evidence that they are wrong about something, they can always lock themselves inside their PIT: Prison of Invincible Thought. It sounds like this: "Say what you like, I know what I saw," or, "Say what you like, I know what I know." There is no successful way to argue against this assertion.

This tendency to accept whatever fits our lens and reject everything else is called confirmation bias.

There are people in the world who, priding themselves on their rational scepticism, try *not* to succumb to confirmation bias. They strive to adopt a more objective lens that is *not* largely fuelled by self-interest and what they may *want* to be true. However, these people are exceedingly rare. Also, they are never 100% successful. A sliver of self-interest will always remain.

The Four Purposes Of A Lens

A person's lens serves at least four purposes.

It gives them a way to understand the world — even if it isn't based on good evidence or sound reasoning.

It provides emotional reassurance. It enables them to think, 'I've figured out how the world works so it's not as puzzling or as scary as it once was'.

It's a source of validation and moral absolution: 'I live my life in a good way, the right way. Also, I belong to the good tribe and most of society's problems are caused by *other* people in one or more of the *other* tribes'.

Finally, it provides a convenient, comfortable and easy alternative to thinking or making some mental effort. In any given situation, the easiest and simplest option is always to just think what you've always thought. Taking a fresh look and (possibly) changing your mind involves mental effort, intellectual honesty and enough emotional energy to admit you were mistaken. It's always easier to not do any of this — in other words, to use your current lens rather than put together a new one.

The Futility Of Informal Arguments

Once you understand how people form their beliefs, it's easy to see why it's hard to change anyone's mind — especially during a casual conversation. Let's say you're at a social event, you meet John and it turns out that he believes in astrology whereas you yourself do not. (If you don't like my using astrology as an example, feel free to substitute any other subject on which you might disagree with someone during an informal chat.)

John has lived his life up to this point and has ended up on a particular square with a particular lens — including the belief that astrology is a legitimate source of useful insights. You have lived your life and ended up on a different square with a different lens. John has his story and you have yours. It should therefore be clear that you're unlikely to change his mind during a single, informal conversation.

First of all, you can't change the life that John has lived up to this point. You have no idea what tapestry of influences caused John to end up believing in astrology. Unless you can dismantle all the causal influences, you won't dismantle the resulting belief. As has often been said, 'You cannot rationally argue out what wasn't rationally argued in'. Secondly, John's lens delivers emotional support and satisfaction that he enjoys and doesn't want you to take away.

If you *try* to change his mind, you may think you're showing how impressively well informed you are about good reasoning and empirical evidence. In fact, all you're demonstrating is how *little* you understand about how people form their beliefs and opinions. Also, you're getting a lot less out of the situation than you could. You're putting up barriers instead of building connections with people. This is the precise opposite of what People Joy is all about.

Your unrequested lecture about astrology will not change John's mind. However, you will give John the distinct impression that you're a smug, arrogant type of person who can't tolerate any beliefs that differ from your own. You will also give John the feeling that there's little value in being in touch with you. This is what countless people 'achieve' with their conversations every day. It's a terrible outcome.

So far, we've looked at how people form their beliefs and arrive at their 'lens'. Now, let's see how this fits in with the People Joy approach to disputes and disagreements.

Disagreement Is Good

Whenever disagreements arise, I suggest you go through the three following steps.

Step one is to realise that disagreement is a *good* thing. It isn't something negative that *has* to involve a winner/loser mentality and lead to division, anger or hate. See disagreement for what it really is: an opportunity to learn and to grow. Think back over your life. Consider all the times you misunderstood something, or were doing something the wrong way. In *every* case, you needed someone to come along, disagree with you and give you better information. No disagreement means no learning or growth.

If people never disagreed, we'd never have invented anything or made any progress. You can't get to cars unless someone disagrees with the idea that horses are the ultimate mode of transport. You can't get to the abolition of slavery unless someone disagrees with the notion that it's all right to own people as property. You can't get to 'The Titanic' unless someone disagrees that you can't build an unsinkable ship... no, wait. Scrap that last one.

Value The Relationship

Step two is to value the *relationship* you have with the other person more than you value the *disagreement* or the chance to win an argument. Some people find this a difficult attitude to adopt.

You can say something along these lines: "Just before we discuss this, let me be clear. What matters to me is my relationship with you and the fact that we're friends / co-workers / neighbours [or whatever]. This matters more to me than [the dispute]. If we're going to fall out over this, then I'd prefer not to talk about it now. Maybe we can discuss it another time. But if we can talk about it peacefully, without falling out, fine. Why don't you go first and explain why you feel the way you do? I'd like to listen."

This approach honestly acknowledges that the disagreement exists. At the same time, you express your belief that (a) disagreement doesn't have to lead to conflict or hate and (b) you don't want it to. You are stating that disagreement can be peaceful and respectful. In some situations, it can even be enjoyable.

DONC Or DOC?

Step three is to identify which type of dispute or disagreement you're dealing with.

- Disagreement Of No Consequence (DONC). You have a chat with a friend at a party. She thinks astrology works. You don't. So what? You could both talk about this for ten hours and it wouldn't make the slightest difference to the world. It's a disagreement of no consequence.

- Disagreement Of Consequence (DOC). This means a disagreement that has significant practical consequences, such as negotiating a difficult relationship or business issue.

Let's look at both of these.

Managing DONCs

DONCS tend to arise during informal, social conversations about ideas. There are no practical consequences. For example, you might talk to someone at a social event and find you disagree about politics, religion, diet, lifestyle, social issues or something else. Here are a few People Joy suggestions about managing DONCs.

First of all, whenever you feel the urge to mention that you disagree about something, take a second to consider whether it *matters* to say that you disagree. There are times when your best course is just to enjoy the conversation. This is not to suggest you should pretend to agree when you don't. I'm saying that in some cases you really don't need to bring up the fact that you disagree. You can let it go, enjoy the flow and let the conversation grow.

If you feel you must mention that you disagree, please don't adopt this attitude: 'You're wrong and I can win this argument because I'm better informed and better at reasoning.'

Here's a better attitude: 'Isn't this intriguing? Throughout my life, I've tried to understand what's real, right and true and I've ended up with opinion A. You've done the same yet reached opinion B. How have we arrived at such different conclusions? I'd love to find out more about how you reached your conclusions.'

I'm not suggesting you necessarily say any of this out loud. I'm just suggesting you adopt this general attitude.

When you get into the discussion, don't try to prove to the other person that they're wrong. You're unlikely to succeed (as we've seen) and even if you did you would annoy them. Instead, be intrigued by the fact that you see life through different lenses and welcome the opportunity to explore the subject together.

When the other person is explaining their point of view, make a mental note of anything you *do* happen to agree with. When it's your turn to talk, mention these points of agreement *first*. Never take part in a discussion simply assuming that you're right or that your view is the only correct one. You don't stop learning until you stop breathing. Every disagreement is a chance to learn and to grow. Welcome the chance to have a learning day and go to bed knowing something you didn't know when you woke up.

Managing DOCs: The RCA Principle

Now let's consider how you might approach a DOC: a disagreement of consequence.

What if you're disagreeing with your flatmate about doing their fair share of chores or paying their share of the bills? Or disagreeing with your spouse about an important aspect of parenting that has lasting consequences? Or discussing a policy at the shop, factory or office where you work that will make a big difference to how things are done and who has to do them?

These discussions generally involve changing a policy or a behaviour. You want to persuade someone to *do* something they currently don't do; to *not* do something they currently do; or do something in a different way.

Here's the People Joy approach. You already know a few things about about having good conversations: value the other person, assess the stress, read the room, be aware of emotional subtexts and the fact that a conversation is never just a conversation. So far, so good. I'll have more to say about persuasion later on in Chapter 16, 'The Joy Of Persuasion'. For now, I want to share a simple but tremendously important principle.

Respect, Connect, Affect

If you want to give yourself the *best possible chance* of successfully persuading someone to modify their behaviour, this is the way to go. It's more successful than any alternative plan.

(1) Start by sincerely *respecting* the other person (OP). Don't *pretend* to do this. Do it for real. Show the OP, by what you say and how you behave, that you respect them. People can sense whether you're sincere or not.

(2) Try to build the best *connection* or relationship that you can with the OP. Look for common interests. Do something kind or generous for them. Set yourself the challenge of putting a smile on their face. Do whatever you can to get to know and understand them and to let them know and understand you.

(3) Having completed the first two steps, you can then try to *affect* the OP's behaviour. Be clear about what you want them to do differently and why. Keep it simple, keep it fair and be open to the fact that your view isn't the only view. Invite feedback and listen carefully.

This is the Respect, Connect, Affect pattern (RCA). It doesn't guarantee that you'll get the result you want but then again neither does any other approach. However, it gives you the best chance of successfully achieving a persuasive result. Someone who is smiling is more likely to agree with you, or to change their behaviour to suit you, than someone who isn't. The more the OP likes you, the more likely they are to accommodate you.

I've often seen people try to be persuasive, in either a social or business situation, and fail terribly because they just didn't go about things the right way. They tried to get to the 'affect' part without the 'respect' or 'connect' parts. This doesn't work and there's no reason why it should. It's like trying to cook the spaghetti before you've put any water in the pan. You have to get things in the right order!

When a DOC arises, you can get exasperated, sound angry and abusive, resort to insults and give yourself permission to disparage another human being. All these behaviours will create a barrier between the OP and yourself. Once this barrier is in place, it's highly unlikely that you will persuade the OP to do anything except dislike you and prefer to avoid you. Aim to build *bridges*, not *barriers*.

Additional DOC Points

Let me share a few more ways to increase your chances of success when handling a DOC.

When you get into the discussion, stay calm. Negative emotions, such as tension, anxiety and anger, make it likely that you'll fail to persuade. Angry faces lose their cases. Angry voices lose their choices. Clarity and calm are the persuader's charm. (Trite sayings that rhyme get quoted all the time.)

Remain open to the possibility that you might be wrong. You might have misunderstood something or have been given incorrect information. I've never seen a negotiation that went *less* successfully because someone thoroughly double-checked their facts first.

Be sensitive to the fact that most people feel *emotional resistance* to the idea of changing behaviour. To carry on doing things the same way is always the easiest and most comfortable option. Emotional resistance to change could be a real challenge for the OP. Do they *fear* something that might happen as a result of the suggested change? Fear is a powerful inhibitor. See if you can make the fear go away. Do they *resent* something about the proposed change that they feel is unfair? Explore why they feel this way.

Be willing to trade. Other people are far more willing to change their behaviour if you're willing to change yours.

If you can make some progress, great. If not, remember the Serenity Key. If you can't achieve any positive change, despite your best efforts, then just accept the fact. It's part of your journey in life to learn that you don't always get what you want.

If you are unable to get what you want, you could decide to see if, in a spirit of revenge, you can make the other person's life worse. Don't do this. It only leads to escalation and intensification. What's more, they might be better at finding ways to annoy or attack you than you are at annoying or attacking them. The revenge path just makes it certain that you'll never resolve the original disagreement.

Don't give up on the OP. Aside from the current dispute, they might have all sorts of good points. Maybe one day they'll be able to help you or vice versa.

Continue to be the best friend, colleague, partner (or whatever) you can be. The better your relationship with the OP, the more likely they are to reconsider their position. They might come to you one day and say, "Listen, I've been thinking about [that old dispute we had]. How about if I..." and then they propose a fresh plan. It's a smart move to create the conditions in which this *might* happen, or is even *likely* to happen, rather than conditions that guarantee it will *never* happen.

Give people opportunities to like you. It increases the chances that they'll one day accommodate you. Of course, you can't just press the 'Like Me' button and always get what you want. Nonetheless, being liked gives you the best chance of being persuasive..

You Can Never Win A Fight

This chapter is about the People Joy approach to disagreement. Here's another point worth bearing in mind: there's no such thing as winning a fight.

If you get drawn into a fight, you basically either win or lose. If you lose, you lose. However, even if you 'win', it's not always a good outcome. Your victory often leaves the other person desiring revenge. You never know when the OP might exact their revenge or what form it will take. Even if this counterstrike never materialises, you have to live with the awareness that it *might*. A desire for revenge is a wild tiger prowling around your life, waiting for a chance to pounce.

Try not to get drawn into fights. If you lose, you lose and you won't like that. If you 'win', you create a Revenge Tiger that you don't want prowling around your life.

I learned a lot about this from my friend Gary Turner, a former mixed martial arts champion with thirteen world championships to his credit in kickboxing, Thai boxing and Ju-Jitsu. He told me that, outside of the ring, he would never get involved in a fight even if someone tried to goad him into it or sneered at him for walking away. His view was that (outside of a professional context) there's no such thing as winning a fight. You just never know what problems the Revenge Tiger will make in your life. It's better to just walk away and know peace. And if people want to jeer and call you a coward? "Let them. I want to sleep easy at night," said Gary. "The stronger man is the one who cannot be goaded or provoked."

Never Resent

No matter what's happened, never *resent* another person. Don't take grudges forward or let bad feelings fester inside you.

Let's say you have disagreed with someone about something and, despite all your efforts, you couldn't make any progress. This is a good reason to be unhappy about that *discussion*. It's not a good reason to be unhappy with that *person*. Remember, the OP is in exactly the same position as you. Every day, they are doing the best they can to muddle through this complicated and often thorny maze of experience we call life.

There are several reasons never to resent another person.

(1) Resenting another human being doesn't achieve anything. As Einstein said, "Holding on to resentment is like carrying an anvil round, everywhere you go, and expecting the other person to get tired." (See the DUCK for more about this.) The negative energy of simmering resentment lives in *you*, not the other person, and its poison seeps into *your* life, not theirs.

(2) The other person could turn out to be tremendously helpful or useful to know on another day and in a different context. Even if this seems unlikely, you've nothing to lose by leaving the door open to this possibility. People can surprise you by transforming from villain to hero. Life has taught me this lesson many times. I've often known people who, while they seemed annoying or unhelpful in one context, later turned out to be extremely helpful and well worth knowing. The truth is that open doors are far more valuable in life than ones that are slammed firmly shut.

(3) Resentment doesn't make any progress. To resent is to prefer stasis over the possibility of progress. It's a policy that says, 'The only way to end this fight is to sustain it.'

Resentment and retaliation are both poor choices because you can't hit someone without them either hitting back (which might hurt) or, if they're unable to do so immediately, making them *want* to hit back at a later date. This could quite possibly be when you least expect it. The alternative to resentment is the personal choice not to live with the poison of resentment inside you and to leave the door open to the possibility of progress and peaceful resolution.

Three Final Points

The Golden Glow

When I'm chatting with friends and a disagreement arises, I often say something like this: "Good! This means we get to enjoy the warm, golden glow of peaceful disagreement." (I've already mentioned this phrase a couple of times in this book.)

I am well aware that this sounds like a strange thing to say. However, in my experience people tend to like it when I say it. For one thing, I'm being sincere. This is genuinely how I feel. Secondly, I'm signalling my strong preference for *peaceful* disagreement. This helps people to relax and gets rid of any tension in the air, which promotes better, more open discussion.

Saying something like this suits my style but I accept that it might not suit yours. However, I'm confident that you can come up with some wording, some way of expressing yourself, that conveys the same basic sentiment.

Role Perception

Here's another important part of handling DONCs.

Consider this scenario. You have met someone at a social event and they believe in something that you don't. Let's carry on using the example of astrology. You may feel inclined to present the sceptical point of view and to argue that there's currently no good scientific reason to believe in any of the main tenets of astrology. If you proceed in this way, you may perceive your own role as 'the well informed voice of reason who can save people from their foolish delusions'. Here's what you need to know: this is only your role *if* the other person *agrees* that it's your role and has actively *asked* for you to play this role.

If they have not done both of these things, then they might see your role rather differently. They might see your role as 'pompous, egotistical twit', or, 'dreary know-it-all who thinks I asked for a lecture when I didn't'. Obviously, neither of these roles are consistent with the spirit of People Joy. You role is only what you and the OP have *agreed* is your role.

The Steak And Ice Cream Principle

Before I end this chapter on disagreement, I want to add a short note about those times when a relationship finally comes to an end. I'm referring to *any* type of relationship, such as people ending their romantic involvement or deciding not to work together.

There is a common tendency in such situations for both parties to *insult* or denigrate the other and *blame* them for the ending of the relationship. In my opinion, this isn't the best way forward.

We all know that in music, it's possible to have two great tunes that harmonise and go together well. Tune 1 is enjoyable on its own. Tune 2 is enjoyable on its own. If you play them at the same time they sound wonderful together. However, you can also have two great tunes that don't go well together at all. If you play Frank Sinatra singing, 'I've Got You Under My Skin', and at the same time play Stevie Wonder singing 'Superstition', you get an unlistenable mess of musical porridge. Whatever greatness lies in either song becomes more or less impossible to appreciate.

When two people in a relationship go their separate ways, they can say, "I'm great, and the other person is great, but we found we just don't go together well." This is the Steak And Ice Cream Principle. Even if you like steak and like ice cream, you wouldn't want them on the same plate at the same time. They don't go together well and, in fact, when you combine them you diminish the appeal of both.

There's no need for blame. There's no need for insulting remarks in either direction. The fact that two people don't harmonise doesn't mean there's anything wrong with either of them.

Roses are red, gold is a prize
We are both great but we don't harmonise

Chapter Summary

This chapter was all about managing disagreements. First of all, we looked at how people arrive at their set of beliefs, their 'lens' on to the world. Then we looked at ways of managing disagreement. The main headings were:

- Belief formation: life through a lens.

- Disagreement is good.

- Value the relationship (more than the disagreement).

- DONC or DOC?

- You can never win a fight.

I concluded the chapter with three additional points:

- The golden glow.

- Role perception.

- The steak and ice cream principle.

The next chapter considers what to do whenever you're dealing with angry people.

DUCK

My 'Sceptic' Days: A Personal Apology

I'd like to include a note of personal apology. In this chapter, I referred to the type of person who goes to a party, meets someone who believes in astrology (for example) and proceeds to explain why they are wrong. There was a chapter in my life when I sometimes did this.

At the time, I was involved in what's referred to as the 'sceptics' movement (the spelling is 'sceptic' in the UK and 'skeptic' in America). I read sceptic magazines, joined sceptic groups and went to sceptics conferences. We believed we were champions of rationality, critical thinking and the scientific method. Our general attitude was that the promotion of rationality, truth and sound reasoning was good for society. I sometimes performed at these conferences. I had a show in which I used magic tricks to simulate 'psychic' phenomena such as spoon-bending and telepathy. I no longer have much to do with this community. These days I refer to myself as a 'recovering sceptic'.

During this chapter of my life, I was often the 'Um, actually' guy at parties. If someone happened to start talking about their belief in psychics, UFOs, dowsing or anything along those lines, I used to say, "Um, actually..." and start explaining why they were mistaken. I apologise to anyone who met me on these occasions. At the time, I hadn't learned much about People Joy. I felt it was more important to parade my 'knowledge' about pseudo-science than it was to love people, appreciate them and make good connections with them.

This is the second apology I've included in this book. There was also one at the end of Chapter 11. Writing books like this is so much easier if one first takes the simple, precautionary step of leading a perfect life of radiant flawless excellence. It is a matter of some regret that I have clearly failed to do this.

Einstein Quotation

In this chapter I mentioned a quotation about resentment and carrying an anvil. I attributed this to Albert Einstein. This attribution is false. The 'quotation' is one I made up, based on another quotation that says, 'Holding onto anger is like drinking poison and expecting the other person to die.' I've seen this attributed to over two dozen people, from Nelsen Mandela to Audrey Hepburn.

The internet is a wonderful invention but doesn't come with 'accurate attribution' as standard. It seems that many people attribute random quotations to Albert Einstein so I thought I may as well follow the trend. However, I won't include any more falsely attributed quotations in this book. After all, this wouldn't be a very nice thing to do. As Shakespeare put it:

> "Make not thy sport to lead good men astray
> With counterfeit decree, less honest show
> For honour's ripped, defiled, made disarray
> By sworn assurance of what is not so."
> (King John, Act III, scene ii)

Swift Quotation

I mentioned the saying, 'you can't rationally argue out what wasn't rationally argued in'. I've seen this idea expressed in various ways and attributed to many different people, from George Bernard Shaw to Benjamin Franklin. According to an excellent article on the Quote Investigator website, all of these variants can be traced back to Jonathan Swift's 1721 'Letter To A Young Gentleman'. He wrote, "Reasoning will never make a man correct an ill opinion, which by reasoning he never acquired."

Sinatra

I briefly mentioned Frank Sinatra's recording of 'I've Got You Under My Skin'. This is one of my favourite examples of the magic of collaboration and I happen to think it's hard to beat. Cole Porter, the greatest writer of popular song of the 20th century, came up with the words and music. Nelson Riddle took care of the arrangement and orchestration in his usual brilliantly ingenious way — including the remarkable decision to include a *bass trombone* solo. Sinatra took care of the singing and swinging.

Porter, Riddle, Sinatra: three musical geniuses, each bringing their own special talent to the party. This is a formidable combination by any standards. I'm sure you have your own favourite examples of what can happen when talented people collaborate. Maybe you'll get to tell me about them one day.

Serenity Key (Extended Version)

In this chapter I mentioned the Serenity Key for the second time: 'Change what you can't accept and accept what you can't change'. I recently saw a slightly extended version that I like: 'Change what you can't accept and accept what you can't change. For things you can neither accept nor change, use witchcraft!'

14. Dealing With Anger

"Anger is an acid that can do more harm
to the vessel in which it is stored than to
anything on which it is poured."

— *Mark Twain*

Progress Check

We've reached the seventh and final section of Part Three! This is all about an aspect of People Joy that many people find rather difficult and challenging: dealing with anger and angry people.

People Joy And Anger

At the start of this book, I made it clear that I have no qualifications as a counsellor or therapist. I'd like to repeat this disclaimer. Nothing in this book constitutes qualified medical, therapeutic, psychological or psychiatric advice. This book is not a substitute for such advice or guidance and should not be regarded as such.

What's the People Joy way to deal with people who are angry? Let me see if I can offer some suggestions based on my own experience.

First of all, let me clarify the type of situation I'm referring to. If you're in a situation where you are in any danger, any threat to your mental or physical well-being, your safety takes priority. What I'm talking about in this section are situations where someone is angry or upset but you are *not* personally in any danger.

Anger Is The Sound Of Pain

In most cases, anger is the sound of pain.

We all start off as a baby lying in a cot. At that stage, we lack any way to solve our own problems. If we want something, such as to be fed, we only have one option: make a loud noise. As we get older, we gain greater ability to do things for ourselves and solve our own problems. Unfortunately, people sometimes run out of steps. Perhaps they try to solve a problem in a few different ways and get nowhere. They reach a point where they've tried everything they can think of but nothing has worked and the problem is still there. As a result, they feel blocked and frustrated.

At this stage, some people stay calm and either decide they don't care or accept there's nothing they can do. However, not everyone has the personal and emotional resources to do this. Some people revert to the first problem-solving strategy they ever learned: make a loud noise. This is what anger is. It's the sound some people make when they feel they have run out of steps or are getting close to that point. It's the sound of someone feeling lost, stuck or exasperated. They are trying to move from pain to pleasure but can't work out how to get there. There's usually some fear involved as well — in the same way that a small child feels scared if it senses that all its normal sources of comfort and protection are absent.

How To Respond: Listener Or Fixer?

So, what's a good People Joy way to deal with an angry person?

(1) Understand what's going on. You're seeing another human being who is in pain. They are upset, frustrated and a little lost.

(2) Play for time. While someone is in a high-anxiety, high-adrenalin state, mixed with fear, it's impossible to negotiate with them or have a meaningful conversation. They are too anxious, too mentally and emotionally distracted to be able to negotiate. The good news is that no one can sustain this high-stress, high-adrenalin state for long. If they try to, they will just pass out. After about twenty minutes, they will shift from this high-adrenalin state to one that's slightly calmer and less anxious. (This was all explained to me by a real-life professional hostage negotiator!)

For this reason, your first step is to play for time. Don't add to the pain the OP is feeling. Don't be a threat or antagonise them. Wait until they pass from the high-adrenalin state to a calmer one. They are then able to think, talk and evaluate options.

(3) Once the OP has reached a more settled emotional state, try to create an environment that's conducive to a good result. See if you can create a situation in which the OP feels safe, comfortable and able to talk. Get rid of distractions (such as your phone). Position yourself where *they* want you: a safe distance away (like an interview) or close (so you can, for example, rest your hand lightly on their forearm). Make it clear to the OP that you have time for them and you're going to take this at *their* pace and *they* set the agenda.

(4) Understand which role the OP wants you to play:

- Listener.

- Problem-solver / Fixer.

If the OP knows which of these two roles they want you to play it's important for you to find out. The easiest way is just to ask. "Do you simply want me to listen or to try to come up with a solution?" If it doesn't feel appropriate to ask this direct question, see what your emotional empathy tells you. If you don't feel sure, choose to be a listener. If the OP wants you to be a problem-solver, they'll tell you.

Being A Listener

To be a good listener, be sincere and listen to *understand* rather than to *judge*. The OP may say some things you don't agree with. This isn't the time to judge or argue. You can argue later on, when the situation isn't so emotionally intense.

If you're playing the listener role, you may feel that you're not achieving much. However, you could be providing a great deal of valuable emotional support. Just by listening to the OP, you may be able to soothe their pain to some extent and help them to feel better. To feel that someone is really listening to you, and making the effort to appreciate how you feel, can have tremendous therapeutic value.

Remember that many people are dealing with problems that don't show up on the outside. To make things worse, they may sometimes feel they have to mask their problems and pretend everything's fine. We live in a world where, unfortunately, many people feel lonely, ignored, unheard or isolated.

Being A Problem-solver Or Fixer

Here are a few notes on being a problem-solver.

Show some respect and sympathy. Don't be tactless and glib. If the OP has been dealing with this problem for some time, you're not going to come up with the answer in two minutes. Don't react as if the problem is rather trite and say, "Well, why don't you just...". Even if you're right, it's not helpful to make the OP feel stupid.

Find out which options or solutions the OP has already tried. In some cases, you may feel that the OP's problem is the same as one you've dealt with before. While this may be true, proceed tactfully. There may be subtle reasons why the solution that worked before, in some other situation, won't work in this case.

If it's appropriate, go into problem-solving mode as described in Chapter 3 (including the PERMIT formula).

If you can think of a solution to the problem, suggest it with patience, tact and respect. If you can't think of a solution right away, see if you can find a way to hold out some genuine hope. For example, mention someone else who might be able to help and whom you'll be able to contact tomorrow or the next day. Alternatively, mention a good, credible source of help or information that the OP hasn't tried yet.

If you truly can't offer any practical help with the problem, then be honest and say so. Even if you can't take away the problem, you may at least be able to help the OP to change how they *feel* about it. See if you can ease the pain or help the OP to see things from a different perspective. Bear in mind that people often imagine the consequences of a given problem are going to be much worse than they actually turn out to be.

Make it clear that the conversation you're having *now* doesn't have to be the last one or the only one. Express your willingness to talk to the OP again whenever they feel they want to.

Responding Without Anger

For People Joy purposes, it's clearly advantageous to be able to deal with angry people. It's also important to be able to manage your *own* anger. If you are aware that you have anger management issues, perhaps you need the help of a trained, qualified therapist. I am emphatically not a therapist. However, in this section I'd like to share a few ideas that you might find helpful.

In my early twenties, I felt angry on a fairly regular basis. This was largely as a result of having stumbled cluelessly into the world of work. The typical fissures and fractures of office life often left me smouldering with sulky dismay, whining indignantly to myself about a range of perceived grievances — one or two of which might even have been real. Just to be clear, I was never a *violent* person. Looking for violence in me is like looking for fury in a butterfly. I was just angry with various aspects of life, as young men often are.

Tides have turned, decades have passed and these days anger is a distant stranger. Though I am far from emotionally inert, I never feel even the slightest twinge of anger about anything. This isn't because I spend my days in paradise. There are still plenty of thorns scattered along life's path. However, at some point my angry circuits crumbled to dust. There were several stages on my journey to this peaceful, rageless state of being. As I've mentioned elsewhere, learning to meditate and to play the guitar (the latter being merely the former with the sound turned up) both helped to soothe my angry circuits into lasting silence. I also heard about the Serenity Key, which I've mentioned a couple of times in this book.

I also came to realise, as the years passed, that just because I had an *opportunity* to be angry didn't mean I had to *take* it. (This echoes what I said in Chapter 2 about 'conparing' yourself to others.) I started to think about options and consequences. Let's say I got blamed at work for something that wasn't my fault. I could see I had an *opportunity* to express anger — perhaps of a self-righteous nature. I knew that letting off some emotional steam might feel good.

However, I realised this wasn't the only consequence. I would also look ridiculous to anyone nearby and get a reputation for being prickly and volatile, which wouldn't do much for office harmony. With experience as my teacher, I started responding to such situations in a rather detached way. I could *see* the chance to display anger but also see that I didn't have to take it. Just because you can *see* a door doesn't mean you have to go through it. I found this rather liberating and realised it was the path to a more relaxed and less stressful life.

Two Sources Of Provocation

I started to apply this realisation — that anger is a choice I don't have to take — to two types of provocation.

The first was *criticism*. We've already looked at this in Chapter 2 but I want to mention it here as well for completeness. As I said, there's never any need to feel angry about criticism. If it's *informed* and *constructive*, it's useful. If it fails either or both of those tests, it's useless. All you can do is peacefully ignore it. You have nothing to do except thank the critic and get on with your day.

A second common type of provocation is any type of *personal* abuse or attack. This generally falls into one of three broad categories: 'I don't like you', 'You're no good' or 'You're an idiot'. This often leads to people feeling the need to push back. We've all seen children in a playground enjoy this type of wise, thoughtful exchange:

"You're stupid!"

"No, I'm not! *You're* stupid!"

Adults sometimes express themselves in a similar way. Alternatively, they may be dismissive of whoever has expressed the insult:

"Who cares what [name] thinks? He's an idiot!"

Neither of these options (push back or discredit) is consistent with the goals of People Joy. There is no part of appreciating and loving other people that involves saying you think they and their opinions are rubbish. Fortunately, neither option is necessary. A far better way to respond is to *decline to engage*.

If someone *attacks* you, or tries to, and you reply *defensively*, you are tacitly accepting the pattern: the OP has *attacked* so you must *defend*.

If you choose *not* to reply defensively, you are withdrawing this tacit corroboration and rejecting the pattern. You are refusing to categorise what was said as an attack. The interesting thing is that declining to reply defensively drains all the power from the insult (and also from the person expressing it). The flame that can't burn anything isn't much of a flame.

It also helps to respond with positive compliments, provided that (a) you're sincere and (b) you won't sound as if you're trying to be either sarcastic or antagonistic.

By refusing to respond *defensively*, you are refusing to define yourself as having been *attacked*. Someone saying they don't like you or your work isn't an attack. It's a person expressing an opinion that they have every right to express. Even if you think it's a misguided or unkind opinion, you don't necessarily need to say so. Meanwhile, you can probably find something nice to say to the OP. At the very least, you can thank them for their honesty. After all, honest criticism helps us all to do better.

Refusal to defend implies there was no attack — and if you weren't attacked, there's no need to get angry. As Abraham Lincoln put it: "Am I not destroying my enemies when I make friends of them?"

Anger Reframing

Here's another idea that might help you to manage your own anger. In Chapter 6, I mentioned a technique called Positive Reframing. You can adapt this technique to modify your response to any given situation. The point is that your *first* emotional response doesn't have to be where you *stay*, in emotional terms. You can talk yourself into moving on to a calmer state of mind.

Here's a simple example. I was once staying at a place near the coast and was happy to be there. The only problem was the screeching of the seagulls. Every morning, a long time before I wanted to wake up, I was woken by the screeching seagulls all over the roof of the flat where I was staying. These noisy, annoying birds and their constant screeching made me feel angry and irritated. I was also painfully aware that there was nothing I could do about it. (Earplugs don't work in a situation like this.) On top of everything else, I was worried that I wasn't getting enough sleep and this might affect the work I was meant to be doing.

After a few minutes of feeling angry, I talked to myself to see if I could change my feelings. I shrugged and said, "They're just seagulls doing what seagulls do. It's not like it's some sort of personal vendetta. And I *have* chosen to stay by the sea which, to be fair, is more their natural domain than mine. I can't expect them to change just to suit me. Anyway, they do look elegant in flight and they can do cool stuff like hovering on thermal currents. Yes, they're screechy but, seeing both sides, they probably don't like some of the noises that *we*, human beings, make. It's not so bad."

This didn't change the reality of the situation. However, it *did* modify my emotional reaction and make it feel like less worth getting upset about. I realised I wasn't going to achieve anything by flooding my system with stress hormones.

You aren't in charge of reality so you can't change it. If you try to, you just feel powerless. You are (to some extent) in charge of your emotions so you *can* change them. When you do so, you're taking a positive action and feel less helpless. If you can't change the *facts*, at least work on how you *feel* about them.

Maybe That's Just What They Need

Here's a small point that I want to mention before bringing this chapter to an end. When I encounter someone behaving in an angry, annoying or unpleasant way, I try to remember a few things. One is that I don't know what pains and problems, trials and trauma that person may have been through in their life. Not all scars are visible from the outside. Also, I don't know what problems they may be dealing with on an almost daily basis or how much stress they have to cope with. What's more, they may not have had some of the privileges and advantages that I've had.

Taking all this into consideration, I sometimes say to myself, "Maybe that's just what they need right now." This isn't about forgiving people in a pious or sanctimonious way. It's about being sympathetically realistic. Perhaps if I had their problems, I'd behave in the same way — or even *worse*. For all I know, the person I'm looking at is exercising admirable *restraint* in the face of serious pressure or provocation.

Coda: Let's Choose To Win

We have reached the end of both Chapter 14 and Part Three of this book. This seems like a good time to offer a suggestion based on all the ideas and principles I've mentioned so far. Here it is:

Let's choose to win.

Suppose you're going to talk to someone and you care about the outcome. Perhaps you want to close a sale, do well at an interview, get someone to change their mind, ask someone out on a date, cheer up a colleague or just enjoy yourself at an event where you don't know many people. These are opportunities to achieve a win for yourself and for whoever you're talking to at the time.

Keep your mind switched on rather than relying on conversational autopilot. Talk to the other person with some life and interest in your eyes. Maybe use the ten-second smile (if appropriate). Allow your facial expression to convey warmth, interest and attention. Offer your attentive energy and be sensitive to the OP's mood and feelings. Convey your awareness of all the glorious treasure waiting to be discovered in their mind, heart and story. Be ready to find the other person's greatness and to share your own.

Don't talk to them with a flat, monotonous tone, devoid of warmth or expression. Use the magic and power of your amazing voice to best effect, offering light, shade and colour. Be sensitive to the chat ratio. Try to avoid hijacking and the other mistakes we looked at earlier. Don't let it be a 'So what?' conversation of zero causation.

Using the tools of positive communication doesn't guarantee success. Life reserves the right to be unfair. However, it does make success a hundred times more likely. I think it's time to stop talking to one another as if we're bored and uninterested. Let's talk to one another with some life, expression, energy, feeling and kindness. Let's regard one another as sufficiently amazing to be worth talking to with a switched-on mind and a touch of loving care. It's time to have the best conversations we can have — ones that lead to good things for us all. It's time for a bit of People Joy.

Let's choose to win.

Chapter Summary

This chapter suggested a few ways of thinking about anger, dealing with angry people and (in some cases) handling your own anger. The main headings were:

- Anger is the sound of pain.

- How to respond: listener or fixer?

- Responding without anger.

- Maybe it's just what they need.

- Let's choose to win.

This brings Part Three of the book to an end. In Part Four, we're going to look at three specific skills: selling, persuasion and cold reading.

DUCK

The Karpman Drama Triangle

With regard to handling situations of anger and conflict, you might like to read about the splendidly named Karpman Drama Triangle, which a psychologist friend told me about. This is a way of modelling situations of conflict and disagreement that identifies three roles people tend to adopt: persecutor, victim or rescuer. I think it's an interesting model and you might enjoy applying it to situations you encounter. As with anything else these days, you can of course find more information online.

Even if you're not greatly interested in this model, you have to love the name. It's worth knowing about so you can casually toss it into the conversation at dinner parties if you want to sound clever. Or if you enjoy being surrounded by blank looks.

Toys Story

In this chapter, I shared a few ideas based on my own journey towards a life free from anger. There was one incident that perhaps more than any other helped me to forget how to be angry. I'd like to share the story here.

It happened during my years in the IT industry. One Saturday morning, I went into the office to finish some work against a tight deadline. While I was there, I met Kathy, one of our tireless angels of sales support. She was a popular, easy-going sort of woman who seemed to breeze through life with low-key unruffled charm. As she didn't normally come in on Saturdays, I asked her why she was gracing the grey, empty cubicles with her presence.

Kathy explained that she'd recently been told off by Tom from the sales department. "Strictly speaking," Kathy explained, "I'm supposed to prepare the prospect calling lists for the sales team by the end of the month which, obviously, was yesterday. Sometimes I get them done a day or two early and sometimes a day or two late. Nobody cares because it doesn't really matter. Tom asked me for his lists yesterday and I said I hadn't done them yet so he started yelling at me in front of the whole office. Gave me a right telling off. *Really chucked his toys out.*"

For the benefit of readers from overseas, allow me to explain. Kathy was using an English colloquial expression that means 'to have a temper tantrum'. The full version would be 'he threw his toys out of his pram' (a baby's stroller or pushchair.)

At the time of this conversation with Kathy, I'd never heard this expression before. I have to say I thought it was utterly hilarious! I still do. What an *excellent* way to conjure up the image of someone having a juvenile tantrum!

Kathy finished her story with a shrug. "So, I've come in today to get Tom's lists done. I don't mind. I was on my way into town anyway. It also means I can give him all the worst, most time-wasting prospects to call, which I expect will put a bit of a dent in his sales and leave him with very little commission this month. What a pity, eh?"

When I heard Kathy's story, I realised something: I never wanted to be the type of person whom others referred to in this way. I never wanted anyone to have cause to say something like, "Well, Ian started to chuck his toys out so we just left him to it." From that point on, I decided never to be the 'prickly' guy or the 'temper tantrum' guy. That brief Saturday morning conversation has cast a long shadow. It steered me towards a less angry, more serene outlook on life. There are still some thorns on the path. These days, I just understand that getting angry about them doesn't help.

Thank you, Kathy.

Part Four: Special Skills

15. The Art Of Selling

"You don't compete on price.
You compete on relationships."

— *Patricia Fripp*

Progress Check

We have reached the fourth and final part of People Joy! This part is all about three special skills:

- The art of selling.

- The art of persuasion.

- The art of cold reading.

In The Interests Of Full Disclosure...

There's one point I need to mention before we go any further. This part of the book is mainly about three skills: selling, persuasion and cold reading. Some of my products and services are based on these skills. For example, people and companies sometimes hire me to teach my course 'The Practical Persuasion Method'. I also sell books on cold reading and sometimes teach cold reading classes.

This being the case, you could be forgiven for thinking this part of the book is a thinly-veiled advert for things I sell.

It isn't.

All of the information in this section stands on its own merits. I've tried to make it useful, helpful and informative. If these chapters lead to a few people hiring me for some training or a class, I won't complain. However, this is honestly not my primary purpose in presenting this part of the book.

I felt this point was worth mentioning. Sometimes, you have to address 'the elephant in the room'.

An Interesting Realm

The art of selling has to be one of the most interesting subjects in the world. You can't be interested in selling without also being interested in everything from human nature to good time management, efficient communication and the science of motivation.

During my decades working in sales, marketing and IT, I helped a vast range of companies to market and sell their goods and services. These companies ranged from large multi-nationals and famous brands to small, local businesses. I enjoyed getting to know each client company and learning about the specific challenges they faced within their various markets. In some ways, selling is always the same, whether it's shoes, sugar or shipping containers. In other ways, every product and market is unique.

Since starting my company about 25 years ago, I've sold my own products and services to clients all over the world. If nothing else, it's certainly been an interesting ride!

People Joy And Selling

This book isn't *specifically* about selling and sales technique. However, if you're interested in selling, I hope you can appreciate that more or less all the ideas in this book can help you to sell more successfully. After all, every sale involves a conversation of one type or another.

If I had to choose three of the best ideas in this book for anyone interest in selling, they would be:

- The mind walk principle.

- The ten-second smile.

- Voice magic.

Later on, there's a chapter devoted to cold reading, which you'll also probably find intriguing and helpful. After all, being able to make *meaningful statements* to a complete stranger is a great way to establish instant rapport.

Four Tales To Tell

In this chapter, I am *not* going to try to teach you how to sell. In fact, quite the opposite. I shall assume that you *already* know the basics of successful selling. For example, I will assume you know about USPs, identifying which problem you can solve for the customer, qualifying prospects, selling benefits rather than features and how to 'sell the sizzle, not the sausage'. What's more, I'll assume you know about sales funnels and what CRM software can do for you.

I'm also going to assume that you have your favourite sales model, such as the SPIN Selling technique pioneered by Neil Rackham, and that you've studied most of the top sales gurus, such as David Sandler, Dan Kennedy, Zig Ziglar, Tom Hopkins, Frank Bettger, Brian Tracy and Wes Schaeffer, 'The Sales Whisperer'.

With all these assumptions securely in place, in this chapter I simply want to share four stories with you. All of these stories are from real life and helped me to learn important lessons about the art of selling. I hope you enjoy these stories and get some value from them.

Story 1: The Impossible Sale

I have put this story first for a reason. Even if you neither like nor read the three that follow, I hope you'll like this one. It contains an important lesson that has made a significant difference to my life, especially since I started selling my own services over 25 years ago.

This is a true story from the 1980s, when I worked in corporate video production. At the time, there was a government initiative called the Youth Training Scheme (YTS), which was intended to help young people to find work. The people in charge regularly commissioned videos to explain how the YTS worked and to show a few of the scheme's success stories.

As you would expect, the company I worked for tried to get some of this highly lucrative video work. When I looked into it, I was informed by a YTS official that we couldn't even be *considered* for this work. Why not? Because we weren't on the list of approved suppliers. Naturally, I asked how we could get on the list. I was told that it would take a long time and we would have to submit enough paperwork to fill the British Library — or at least that's what it sounded like. It seemed clear that it was *impossible* for us to get any of this work.

A few months after these discussions, it so happened that the YTS people wanted six videos made in the Leicestershire area, where my company was based. To our surprise and delight, we were invited to pitch and got the contract!

My main YTS contact, who came on all the shoots, was called Terry. As our work on these videos drew to a close, I felt I knew him well enough to ask him a question. "Listen, Terry," I said, "we're pleased that you chose us to make these videos. But can I ask you something? We were told we couldn't even be *considered* for this work as we weren't on the approved suppliers list. So, what happened?"

Terry smiled and gave a little shrug. "Ah, yes, the good old approved suppliers list. Well... *I decided to ignore that.*"

This is when I learned a valuable lesson. The fact is, if people *want* buy your products or services, they'll find a way to do so. They'll either justify it afterwards somehow or simply ignore their own policies *when it suits them*. All experienced sales people know this. This is how they manage to make 'impossible' sales all the time!

Story 2: The Secret Of Rick's Success

Here's an interesting true tale about successful selling.

I once worked for an IT company in north London. We had about a dozen full-time sales staff, all of whom were pretty good at their job. However, one person on the sales team consistently out-performed all the others. I'll call him Rick (not his real name). Almost every month, he was the company's best salesperson. The reasons for his success were something of a mystery within the company.

One evening, during a company social event, I found myself with Rick at a quiet table in the corner of a bar. I took the opportunity to ask him about the secret of his success. At the time, Rick was savouring a particularly nice glass of red wine. Replacing his glass on the table, Rick smiled at me and gave a shrug.

"Okay," he said, "I'll tell you. But there's really not much to it. Last Wednesday, I made a sales visit to [name of company] and spoke with Jim, their head of IT Systems. As I chatted with him, I learned that he had only been doing the job for a couple of months. He and his wife has moved quite a long way across the country so he could take up this new job. It had been a time of upheaval: new location, new house, new job.

"I asked him how it was going. Jim said it was mostly all right... but there was one problem. His wife has been supportive of the move and knew it was the right thing to do. However, her great passion was horse-riding. At their old place, where they used to live, there was a private stables that was only half an hour's drive away. She used to go riding there, with a few of her friends, once or twice a week. However, now that Jim and his wife had relocated, she couldn't go riding any more."

This story took place many years before the glorious invention of the internet. Getting information wasn't as simple as searching online for whatever you want to know.

"I made a note of Jim's problem. Well, more specifically, his *wife's* problem. I know a *lot* of people and, in the days after that sales visit, I made several dozen phone calls. I asked everyone I could think of about stables and horse-riding. There were a lot of dead ends but, eventually, I was able to get some useful information.

"I called Jim on the phone. I told him that I'd found a friend of a friend who knows the owner of a stable where they have a weekly riding club. It was about forty minutes from Jim's new home. I added, 'I've talked to one of the women who goes there every Thursday and, as it happens, you aren't far out of her way. She'd be happy to pick up your wife and drive her there. Also, I've had a word with the stable owner and your wife can have her first month's membership free to see if she likes it. I'll send you all the details.' "

Rick finished telling me the story. He leaned back in his chair and took a sip of his wine.

"Now then, Ian," said Rick, "next time Jim needs some software or a new tech support deal, who do you think he's going to call?"

That was Rick's 'secret', if you can call it that. He saw it as part of his role to get to know his clients and to note *any* way in which he could do them a favour or maybe solve a problem for them. Rick saw his customers as *people* with a range of wants, needs and problems. He made the effort to be their friendly and effective problem-solver.

Story 3: What Jenny Knew

This story is similar to the previous one but I felt it was too good to leave out.

Back in my video production days, in the 1980s, I made several videos for a national pharmaceutical company. They employed several dozen sales reps, each tasked with selling the company's products to all the chemist shops (drug stores) in their allocated region of the country.

At the time of this story, the company's newest sales rep was a petite young woman called Jenny. Most of the other sales reps were men. Some of these men made rather derogatory remarks about Jenny behind her back. They insinuated that she probably wouldn't last long in the tough, competitive world of selling. To their surprise and dismay, Jenny consistently achieved top sales figures.

Jenny's company organised a large sales conference at a luxury hotel on the south coast. My company had produced about a dozen videos for the conference, which is why I happened to be there (along with the rest of the crew). I got along well with Jenny and one afternoon, during a lull in the conference proceedings, I had a chat with her over coffee in the lobby of the hotel. Her outstanding sales record had already been mentioned once or twice during the conference so, naturally, I asked her about it. How had she managed to out-sell her (mostly) male colleagues?

"Ah well," Jenny replied with a conspiratorial tone, "it's because I know something they don't."

"And what would that be?"

Jenny said she'd tell me provided I didn't tell anyone else. As roughly forty years have elapsed, I believe it's all right to share the story.

From the depths of her cavernous handbag, Jenny extracted a small notebook with a blue cover. Inside, there was one page devoted to every pharmacist in her area. On each of these pages, Jenny had made a note of the pharmacist's wedding date and birthday. She also had the names, ages and birthdays of all their kids.

"When I first visit a chemist," Jenny explained, "I get all of this information. Then, whenever I call on them, I check my book first. When I visit, which is usually at a time when they're not too busy, I say something like, 'Are you looking forward to Harriet's birthday on Tuesday? Seven years old... she's quite a big girl now! By the way, I got her a little birthday card.' Or I say, 'So, are you taking Caroline somewhere nice for your wedding anniversary on Saturday?' "

"And that's how you sell more than the others?" I asked.

"Yes. You see, the others go in and deliver a sales pitch, which is boring. I go in and talk to the pharmacist about *themselves* and their family. My job isn't to sell twenty cases of our latest product. My job is to be someone the customer *likes* and feels they can *trust* like they'd trust a friend. So, when we *do* talk about business, if I say our new product is good, we're running a big ad campaign and there's going to be plenty of demand for it, they trust me and place a big order."

Jenny tucked the notebook back in her bag and sipped her coffee. "I told you, I know something the other sales reps don't: *the birthdays of my customers' kids.* Most of the other reps, by which I mean the men, don't even know the birthdays of their *own* kids!"

Story 4: Brian's Golden Question

When I worked in IT, I had a superb manager called Brian. He had a background in retail sales and knew all there is to know about how to sell. From time to time, I'd take Brian out for lunch and chat about sales, selling and what his experience had taught him. One day, I remember, Brian mentioned what he called 'the golden question'. He told me that he had learned to always ask every customer, "What do you *really* want?"

As Brian explained, people don't want to buy a mop. The mop is just a means to an end. What they *really* want is to have nice, clean, shiny floors. People don't really want to buy a train ticket. The ticket is just a means to an end. What they *really* want is a reasonably comfortable way to reach their destination. You get the idea.

Asking customers what they *really* want is a simple yet effective way to expand one's sales opportunities. The truth is, customers don't always have the full picture or know what options are available. They sometimes make assumptions about what you can or can't do for them. When they tell you what they *really* want, you may find you can offer a better solution than the one they had in mind.

During my years with the IT company, this point came up all the time. Some customers assumed that our software came as a 'standard' package, meaning they just had to accept whatever it could or couldn't do. They hadn't realised that we could *customise* our software to meet all of their requirements. This raised the price but was still cost-effective from their point of view. Your product is only a means to an end. Find out where the customer is trying to get to and then help them get there.

This point often comes up in my own work, for example when people hire me to speak at their conference (blatant plug). They sometimes *assume* that they have to choose between information or entertainment; a talk or a show. The truth is that, once I'm at an event or conference, they can have as much or as little of me as they want. For example, when I was hired to train FBI agents, I first of all presented a full day of training (largely about cold reading and persuasion). Later, in the evening, we all went to an Italian restaurant and, at their request, I performed a short after-dinner magic show!

Always ask Brian's golden question: "What do you *really* want?"

Some Free Ideas

On my website (ianrowland.com/peoplejoy) you can find a number of completely free booklets available as instant downloads. One of these, 'Smart Communication Tips', contains several ideas and techniques that you'll like if you're interested in selling. These include 'Conversation Tracking' (a way to *genuinely* read someone's mind), 'The Comfort Formula', 'Pre-emptive Neutralisation' and 'Supply The Mnemonic'. It's a short, easy-to-read booklet, instantly available and completely free.

I have another free booklet called 'Stories To Learn From' that you might also like. It's a selection of business-related tales from real life that illustrate important lessons.

Chapter Summary

This chapter consisted of four stories that I think shed some light on the fascinating art of selling. The main headings were:

- A fascinating realm.

- The secret of Rick's success.

- What Jenny knew.

- Brian's golden question.

- The impossible sale.

The next chapter deals with the subject of persuasion. I *urge* you to read it as it will only be available *for a short time* and everyone who reads it will be entered into a *prize draw* to win a *luxury holiday!*

16. The Art Of Persuasion

"Yet a greater, unlearned skill he possessed,
which was the art of kindness."

— Ursula K. Le Guin

Progress Check

This is Part Four of People Joy. It predominantly concerns three specific skills: selling, persuasion and cold reading. The preceding chapter featured four stories about selling. Now, we can look at the intriguing art of persuasion.

We Are All Persuaders

We all want to be successful persuaders from time to time. Whether you want to persuade someone to give you a job, go on a date, sign a deal, follow a new policy, tidy their room, buy your product, work an extra shift, sign a Nuclear Arms Treaty or buy this book, we all have an interest in the psychology of persuasion.

This book isn't specifically about persuasion. However, I've included this chapter for two reasons. The first is that, as I've said, we all sometimes have conversations in which we'd like to be persuasive, so I felt it was relevant. The second reason is that persuasion is one of my favourite subjects. I love learning about it and teaching it. Over the years, I've had a lot of interesting adventures teaching persuasion skills to various people and companies.

In this chapter, I'm not trying to offer a comprehensive theory of persuasion. My only aim is to share seven useful principles. None of these principles are successful *all* the time. All of these principles are successful *some* of the time.

(Incidentally, I have a course called the 'Practical Persuasion Method' or PPM for short. There are more details in the DUCK.)

1. ATD

This stands for 'Avoid Triggering Defences'.

If you push someone, they tend to push back. Similarly, if you *blame* anyone for anything or claim they're at fault, they tend to defend themselves by arguing that in fact *you* are to blame. These are natural and largely instinctive reactions. Once you have triggered someone's defences, you'll find it virtually impossible to persuade them to do anything or to change their mind. In fact, you'll achieve the opposite result. They will feel more determined than they were before to resist your request or suggestion.

If you want to be persuasive, ATD is a good initial strategy that stimulates creative thinking. It encourages you to find a way to *frame* a persuasive conversation in a way that avoids triggering the other person's defences. I'm going to mention three practical frames that are often effective.

You're Probably Not Aware

Start from the position that the other person (OP) is decent and considerate but just not *aware* that what they're doing is annoying or problematic. (Even if you suspect they are in fact *perfectly* aware, this is a good persuasive starting point.)

Suppose you live in a shared house and John likes to play loud music, often when you're trying to concentrate or get some rest. Here's the wrong approach: "Hey, stop being such an inconsiderate moron! Turn your music down or I'll smash those speakers to pieces. I'm trying to get some rest."

Here's a better way: "Hi, that's pretty cool music! Can I just mention something? You're probably unaware of how much your music can seep through the walls and echo around this place. I guess these old flats aren't very sound-proofed! I don't mean to complain but I know you're very considerate so I just thought I'd mention it. I have to be up early tomorrow and I'm trying to get an early night if I can."

This approach doesn't trigger John's defences. Instead, it gives him an *opportunity* to demonstrate that he's considerate by turning his music down. He may or may not take this opportunity. However, it's a better strategy than calling him names and making threats.

Let's Work Together

Here's another way to avoid 'pushing' someone and triggering their defences. Say you'd like to work *with* the OP to address whatever the issue happens to be. In other words, express your interest in collaboration. "Hi John. Listen, you like playing your music loud and you've every right to. It's okay. I want you to enjoy your music. But I really need to get some sleep because I'm on these crazy shifts and I have to be up by 6am. So I wanted to just have a chat and see if there's a way we can both get what we want. I know you often come up with good ideas. Can we work something out?"

Maybe John will suggest a system whereby you let him know when you need an early night and when you don't. Alternatively, and for future occasions, he may suggest that if you contribute to the cost of some headphones, he'll use them. Whatever the outcome, you'll get a better result than simply yelling at John for being selfish.

The Hero Offer

Here's a third way to avoid triggering the OP's defences. It involves a neat bit of reverse psychology.

Let's say you are at the check-in desk at the airport. You're nice and early so they aren't particularly busy. You have purchased a normal, economy class ticket but would like an upgrade. One approach is simply to ask: "Is there any chance of an upgrade? I bet you could find a way if you really wanted to. Is there anything you can do?"

In this scenario, there is no *incentive* for the assistant behind the desk to help you. Even if they succeeded, they would have done nothing except succumb to your will. Their only role in this scenario is 'servant who did your bidding'. Consider this alternative:

"Thank you. By the way… remind me, how long's the flight?"

"Three hours."

"Wow. That's going to be a bit rough for me. My psoriatic arthritis is playing up and my legs are sore. I've tried premium class before and I know the seats have a bit more leg room. But it's all right. I know there's nothing you can about it and I'm *not* asking you to. I guess I'll manage. Have a nice day. "

You have now given the OP something they didn't have before: *the opportunity to be a hero*. They can be the brilliant fixer who saves the day and turns the situation around. Assuming they *do* have some room for manoeuvre, they might say something like:

"Well, hang on a moment. Maybe there is something I can do. I'll have to check but I'm pretty sure premium isn't fully booked. Leave it with me and I may be able to sort something out."

You can apply the same idea to many other situations. Suppose you ask someone a favour and, because of your tone, it *sounds* to them almost as if you're ordering them to comply. The only way for them to push back, to assert their power, is to *deny* you what you want.

Alternatively, suppose you offer polite, pleasant acceptance and submission. You say you know they can't do anything, you understand, and you're neither asking nor expecting them to. In this case, they have a different way to assert their status and power. It's also a chance to wrap themselves in glory. It's as if you're inviting them to respond in a rather defiant way and say, "Oh, you think I can't do anything? Well, we'll see about that! Maybe I can do more than you think!"

In this case, their *defiance* (of your expectations) works in your favour so you might get what you want. I've found this to be a surprisingly useful and effective strategy. If ever you want to be bored for an hour, ask me to tell you a few stories about the times and places when I've used this approach.

I have made it clear that these three versions of ATD won't be successful in *every* situation. However, they work more often that anger, threats and insults or any attempt to *blame* the other person.

This concludes 'Avoid Triggering Defences', the first of my seven persuasive principles. Let's move on to number two.

2. The RCA Principle

This stands for 'Respect, Connect, Affect'. I covered this principle in the chapter on disagreement but I wanted to include a recap in this chapter for completeness.

To be persuasive, first of all *respect* the other person (OP). Be sincere and respect the fact that they may have a different opinion from you.

Secondly, *connect* with them. Build a bridge over to their world. Create some sort of relationship, even if it's quite a limited one. Find one or two things you have in common. Obviously, your ability to do this will be governed by the context, how much time you have and the social customs in your part of the world.

Thirdly, try to *affect* how the OP thinks or feels about the situation you want to discuss. Be civil, respectful and good-natured, and present your case or your request as simply as you can.

When people fail to be persuasive, it's usually because they jump straight to the 'affect' part. This is simply a case of getting things in the wrong order, like trying to drive a car before you've put any fuel in it. It never works and there's no reason why it *should* work.

3. The PEG Principle

'PEG' stands for 'Perceived Emotional Gain'.

People are constantly trying to move towards what feels good and away from what feels bad. Every decision, every choice, every purchase someone makes is fundamentally an attempt to achieve an improved emotional state. It's true that people sometimes try to think and behave rationally. However, for the most part, they experience life through their feelings and emotions. At any given time, especially when there's a choice to be made, their emotions govern their choices, behaviour and responses. This being so, a good persuasive strategy is to offer the other person a *perceived emotional gain*.

If you can shape your persuasive message so that it offers the other person a PEG, you are likely to succeed. If you can't, you are likely to fail — which is entirely understandable. Why would anyone choose an option that makes them less happy, content or fulfilled than they were in the first place?

PEGS Can Take Many Forms

An 'emotional gain' can take many different forms. Here are a few of the things that, from the OP's point of view, might constitute a PEG: feeling safe and secure; feeling that choice X makes life easier; feeling listened to and involved; feeling validated; feeling that they are part of the 'winning' group or tribe.

A few more options: feeling smart and intelligent; feeling cared about or loved; feeling that you've given them elite status; feeling that they got a special bargain; feeling important and powerful, with things being arranged just to suit them. This list could go on forever.

Though a PEG can take many forms, you have to find one that appeals to the other person. What you think they *ought* to like or find appealing is irrelevant. There's no point offering someone a PEG they don't want, don't care about or feel they can achieve without your help. For this reason, you need to ascertain, as best you can, the PEG that the OP will find most appealing. A good way to do this is simply to *listen* to the OP. In most cases, the type of PEG someone wants isn't a dark secret that they keep to themselves. They'll happily tell you. All you have to do is listen.

The Easiest PEG Is Preferred

If someone has two choices, both offering a PEG, they will choose whichever option is easier. In other words, they will take the option that involves the least time, effort, hassle, complexity and conditions. This isn't because people are lazy (or at least this isn't necessarily the reason). It's just that people are wired up to be efficient. Every monkey reaches for the nearest banana.

For this reason, being persuasive isn't *just* about offering a PEG. If you're competing with another persuader or another option, you have to make sure you're offering the *simplest, easiest* path to a PEG. Many companies are aware of this principle but not all of them. If it is significantly easier to book a room in my hotel than in yours, with far fewer stages involved and a lot less form-filling, then (all else being equal) I'll get more bookings.

4. Simplicity Wins

In order for someone to act on a message or suggestion, they have to be able to do two things:

- Understand it.

- Remember it (unless it's an 'instant decision' scenario).

With regard to both of these points, simplicity works for you while complexity works against you. Many attempts to be persuasive fail because the message you're trying to get across is complicated, hard to understand and hard to remember. Short, simple messages work best. In my career, I've been involved in the sales and marketing plans of a huge number of companies. In many cases, one of the first things I did was review all their publications (point-of-sale material, ads, printed brochures and so on) and show them how to make their key messages easier to understand and to remember.

Simplicity is not the *only* factor that matters. You have to achieve the ideal balance between simplicity and sufficient detail. Having worked as a writer-for-hire, I'm acutely aware of this issue (see the DUCK for a fuller account). My point is that, all else being equal, you should try to harness the power of simplicity so your message is easy to (a) understand and (b) remember.

5. The Power Of Enthusiasm

If you want to persuade, sincere and well founded enthusiasm helps a lot. Being enthusiastic doesn't guarantee you will be persuasive. However, *not* being enthusiastic guarantees you will *not* be.

Let your enthusiasm for your message show in your energy, body language, eyes and tone of voice. You can do this in a nuanced and subtle way. Nonetheless, let your enthusiasm glow and shine. When you enthuse, you're hard to refuse. The enthusiasm has to be sincere and well founded. If someone asks why you're enthusiastic about (whatever the subject is), you have to be able to offer credible reasons. Merely putting on a fake 'Look how enthusiastic I am!' happy face won't achieve much.

Enthusiasm is important in job interviews. If you have genuine enthusiasm for the job, and you can explain why, you will greatly increase your chances of getting hired. If you aren't enthusiastic about the job, no one will feel enthusiastic about giving it to you.

The power of an enthusiastic attitude to win people to your cause was understood even in Shakespeare's time. As he expressed it:

> *"The quickened pulse, with keen and brighter eye*
> *Conveys resolve and fierce aspiration*
> *Inspires the loyal hand, the battle cry*
> *True hearts aligned in single declaration."*
> (A Winter's Tale, Act III, scene ii)

6. Pre-emptive Neutralisation

When you're striving to persuade or sell, there's often a particular objection that the other person has thought of (or soon will). This objection or suspicion is like a little goblin, flitting around in their mind and threatening to undermine all your attempts to sway their thoughts and choices. Until you've managed to deal with this annoying goblin, it's impossible for you to persuade or sell successfully. The goblin is too much of an intrusive distraction.

There's one golden rule: you have to mention the objection *first*, before the OP does, and disarm it effectively. If you fail to do so, the OP might well get the feeling that you're trying to deceive them or at least conceal the bigger picture — and who can blame them? You have to burn the objection before it burns your message. This is called pre-emptive neutralisation.

Consider someone selling a TV. He says to the customer, "Based on what you've said, I think you'd be really pleased with this [brand] widescreen model." The customer replies, "It does look good. Then again, you might just be saying that because it's the most expensive one, so you get a bit more commission."

At this point, there's not much the salesperson can say to rescue the situation. The damage has been done.

Here's the more successful approach. "Based on what you've said, I think you'd be really pleased with this [name of brand] widescreen model. It's true that it's among the more expensive options but that's honestly not why I'm recommending it. If I felt you'd be just as happy with one of these [gestures to less expensive TV sets] I'd say so. But the fact is that this set gives you [mentions several features the customer wants]."

Pre-emptive neutralisation is a good way to increase your chances of persuasive success. All you have to do is ask yourself, before the conversation, is there an objection or suspicion that's likely to occur to the OP and derail your attempt to persuade them? If so, you need to bring it up *before* they do and deal with it.

7. Benign Authority

We all tend to dislike bossy authority figures who tell us what we can and can't do — even if we understand they are just doing their job. However, there's a different type of authority figure that we all tend to *love*. I'm referring to benign authorities — people whose expertise can make problems disappear. We all like the person who can repair the car or get the computer to do what we want. We naturally warm to people who say, "I can fix that for you."

This response is a fundamental aspect of human nature. It's part of how we bond with our parents. It's also part of our tribal instinct to trust elders and those whose wisdom, based on experience, could help or protect us. On another level, it also reflects a basic human drive to solve problems as easily (and perhaps lazily) as possible. It's always easier to use someone else's knowledge than to gain that knowledge yourself. For all these reasons, it can often assist your persuasive efforts to play the role of the benign authority figure.

Back in the days when I was involved in video production, I knew a salesman who went round production companies selling cameras and related equipment. His approach was to say, "In your line of work, you need to know what the latest technology and equipment can do. It will help you to make some informed choices next time you're buying new equipment. Give me twenty minutes and I'll give you a quick rundown of all the latest gear and what it can do, and then I'll leave you alone."

In reality, he was simply pitching his company's products. However, he *positioned* himself as a benign authority figure, someone whose knowledge (about all the latest equipment) could be really useful to the production companies he visited. This approach worked well and he was highly successful.

If you want people to like you, play the part of a benign authority.

Chapter Summary

In this chapter, I outlined seven persuasive principles:

- ATD (avoid triggering defence).

- The RCA Principle (respect, connect, affect).

- The PEG Principle (perceived emotional gain).

- Simplicity wins..

- The power of enthusiasm.

- Pre-emptive neutralisation.

- Benign authority.

The next chapter is all about the curious world of cold reading.

DUCK

My PPM Course

I have a course called the 'Practical Persuasion Method' (PPM). The material in this course is not the same as the material in this chapter. In the PPM, I start by presenting a new and comprehensive model of persuasion. I then invite attendees to suggest real-life situations in which they'd like to be more persuasive. These are usually work-related although sometimes people bring up personal or social situations. I then lead the group analysis of the situation and, referring to the model I've already presented, explore how one might achieve the desired persuasive result. I don't necessarily have any advance notification of the scenarios that people put forward.

I've taught this course to a broad range of individuals, companies and organisations. If you'd like more information, please refer to my website (ianrowland.com/peoplejoy).

A PEG Problem

I mentioned aiming to provide a perceived emotional gain that will interest whoever you're talking to. However, there is one slight complication: people don't always understand their own responses. They may not know which rational or emotional factors are guiding their decisions.

In one study, professional recruiters were asked to list which factors guided their hiring decisions. They *believed* they made decisions based on rational factors, such as each candidate's qualifications and relevant experience. In fact, there was no correspondence, in statistical terms, between these factors and their actual choices. When the statistics were analysed, the single most critical factor was simply 'pleasantness'. It really came down to whether or not they *liked* the applicant. (Higgins & Judge, 2004, 'The Effect of Applicant Influence Tactics on Recruiter Perceptions and Hiring Recommendations'.) This is from Richard Wiseman's brilliant book, '59 Seconds'.

All of Richard Wiseman's books are excellent and well worth reading. He's a superb writer and speaker and clearly an expert in his field. I particularly recommend 'Quirkology' and 'Paranormaility: Why We See What Isn't There'.

The Detail Dilemma

Earlier in this chapter, I wrote, "You have to achieve the ideal balance between simplicity and sufficient detail. Having worked as a writer-for-hire, I'm acutely aware of this issue." If you wonder what I meant by this, here's a small slice of autobiography for you. There's no need whatsoever to read this section and if you prefer you can simply skip ahead to the next chapter.

Back in the 80s, I worked for a place that made corporate videos. At the time, we needed a truck full of clunky, expensive equipment to actually shoot the material. We also needed a room full of clunky, expensive equipment to edit the footage into something vaguely coherent. The result was slightly less good than videos you can now make on your phone. Yesterday's 'cutting edge' tech is always the caterpillar to today's butterfly.

Let me emphasise that, for the most part, I really enjoyed this chapter of my career. The clients were good to work with and I genuinely enjoyed helping people to say what they wanted to say as well as it could be said.

However, one part of the job was slightly annoying. Let's say I'd been asked to write a promotional video. I would do the research, interview a few people and then write the first draft. The next step was to trot along to the client's office and present the script for approval. Typically, I'd find myself sitting in a boardroom with the Head Of Marketing plus two or three of her minions.

After I'd gone through the script, these minions felt they had to say something in order to justify their existence. This being so, I knew they were likely to accuse me either of having included too much detail or too little.

Suppose I had written a fairly simplified script, aiming to make it punchy, easy to understand and memorable. One of the minions would adopt the tone of a shrewd philosopher sharing his profound analytical judgment with the room. He would say, "The script may be all right as far it goes. However, I feel you've missed out quite a number of important details, including some of our key marketing messages. I mean, if the video isn't getting these key messages across, then quite frankly, what's the point? It scarcely seems worth bothering with. Details matter."

Alternatively, suppose I had written a script that *did* include these desperately important details. In this case, the philosopher would say, "The script may be all right as far as it goes. However, it goes into an awful lot of detail and, quite frankly, I doubt the average viewer will be able to take it all in. I mean, I thought you were supposed to be good at simplifying things? It's meant to be a sales video, not a documentary. It needs a bit of zing and impact!"

As you can imagine, I was filled with gratitude for these precious insights into how to do my job.

Duly inspired to try harder, I went away and prepared a second draft of the script. This would be subject to the same 'too much / too little' criticism, even if it flatly contradicted everything said at the previous meeting. Learning to negotiate these chicanes of whimsical critique was an important part of my early career as a writer.

Anyone reviewing non-fiction writing can say there's either too much detail or too little. It's the easiest type of 'criticism' to offer, requiring neither thought nor comprehension. It barely even requires a brain stem. You could simply flip a coin with 'too much' written on one side and 'too little' on the other. Alternatively, you could place two sets of cat treats on the floor of the boardroom, some distance apart. Next to one of them, put a sign saying 'too much detail'. Next to the other, put a sign saying 'not enough detail'. Bring a cat into the room, place it in the middle and see which set of treats it goes to first. This is an excellent way to resolve boardroom disputes or make important strategic decisions.

Feel free to write and inform me that this book errs either on the side of too much detail or too little. It would be fun to end up with two stacks of emails and letters, one half in the 'too much' pile and the other half in the 'too little' pile. I shall enjoy agreeing emphatically with *both* sets of correspondents.

17. The Art Of Cold Reading

*"The greatest good you can do for
another is not just share your riches,
but reveal to them their own."*

— Disraeli

Progress Check

So far in Part Four we've looked at two specific skills related to People Joy: selling and persuasion.

Now we can look at a third skill: the amazing and fascinating art of cold reading.

An Incredible Art

Cold reading is the greatest conversational skill in the world. It's also the greatest persuasive technique you can learn and the nearest thing to real magic that this world has to offer. When you develop cold reading proficiency, you immediately have:

- The greatest rapport-building technique in the world, which is especially useful if you're interested in selling.

- Greater insight into human communication than you can obtain in any other way.

- A few cool party tricks, such as being able to talk to a complete stranger as if you've known them all your life!

Cold reading is a vast subject. In this chapter, I can't cover it in any sort of comprehensive detail. My aim is simply to tell you what cold reading is, dispel a few myths and explain the basic techniques involved. I'll also talk about why it's useful in everyday life and in business (for example, if you want to sell, persuade or negotiate). I've written three books on different aspects of cold reading, from which you may conclude that I'm *slightly* obsessed with the subject. In this chapter, I hope I can convey my love for this amazing conversational art and encourage you to study it further.

A Working Definition

There are various ways to define cold reading. My favourite definition is simply this:

How to talk to people as if you're psychic.

Let me provide some context. Every year, millions of people go for 'psychic' readings of one type or another. For example, they might go for a reading based on tarot cards, their astrological chart, the lines on the palm of their hand, the I Ching (very popular throughout Asia) or some other traditional belief system.

I'll call the person who gives the reading the 'reader' and the person they give it to the 'client' (whether or not they pay any money). Let's assume they are complete strangers. The intriguing part is that the reader can make seemingly correct statements about the client's personality, life, experience, feelings and future. The reader might also mention highly specific details the client can relate to, such as the name of a close friend or a recent event that took place at work.

There are two ways to account for this phenomenon. One is to believe that psychic powers are real, tarot cards work, astrology delivers useful insights and so on. The alternative is to say the reader is good at cold reading.

You may wonder why it's called 'cold reading'. Within the psychic industry, a 'hot' reading is one that involves secretly obtaining information about the client beforehand. There are many sneaky ways to do this. Cold reading is the opposite: giving a reading when you're starting 'cold', so to speak, *without* any advance information. Personally, I have little interest in hot reading. For me, cold reading is a far more fascinating and useful technique.

While we're defining terms, I ought to mention that the term 'cold reading' is sometimes used in the acting profession. It refers to reading a script 'cold', without any preparation. This chapter has nothing at all to do with actors or acting.

My Cold Reading Journey

I thought it might provide a bit of context for this chapter if I briefly summarised my involvement with cold reading. By all means skip this section if you prefer.

My interest in cold reading dates all the way back to my teenage years when I began studying magic and related fields. As the years passed, and I stumbled my way through life's twisted maze of whys, highs and sighs, I continued to learn all I could about this fascinating art. I also gave *lots* of readings (based on tarot, astrology, palms or whatever). It became clear that giving someone a reading can be a wonderful way to brighten their day, boost their confidence or make them feel special and important. I've never met anyone who didn't welcome and enjoy the experience.

I've sometimes demonstrated cold reading for journalists and the media. For example, I once took part in a BBC documentary called 'Heart Of The Matter'. They asked me to give astrological readings to two women I'd never met before. I just made the readings up, based on no astrological 'data' whatsoever. The first woman said my reading was '95% accurate' while the second said it was '99.5% accurate'.

On another occasion, ABC TV asked me to demonstrate spiritualism (relaying messages from the dead) for a 'Primetime' Halloween special presented by Diane Sawyer and Chris Cuomo. I worked with an invited audience of about 20 complete strangers. Most of them said the messages I gave were meaningful and included accurate, factual details. Chris Cuomo then led a discussion during which he tactfully and sensitively admitted that this segment had been about cold reading and how we all form our beliefs. Nobody's feeling were hurt and nobody left feeling fooled or conned.

These days, I give readings whenever a suitable opportunity presents itself. For example, when I take part in shows at The Magic Circle, I sometimes give readings during the interval and after the show. I've taught aspects of cold reading to many people and companies and have also run cold reading classes in London.

Using cold reading to simulate 'spiritualism' for ABC Primetime

Important Clarifications

I'd like to clarify a couple of things. First of all, I have never charged money for a reading or wanted to. To my mind, charging for a reading gets rather murky in ethical terms. Also, I've often given readings in informal situations where it would have been odd to ask for money.

Secondly, I have never claimed to have any psychic ability. It's true that I put 'psychic' in the title of my book 'Super Psychic Readings', which I mention in the DUCK. This was just so that people would know what it's about. In real life, when I give readings, I never mention the word 'psychic'. I call them 'personal' readings instead, which I think is a better description. It's also less likely to provoke wretchedly dull arguments about whether psychic abilities are real. (Answer: they are as real as you want them to be.)

Four Misconceptions

There are several misconceptions about cold reading that are baseless yet unhelpfully persistent. I think it's useful to get these out of the way before discussing how cold reading *actually* works. I apologise for the length of this section but I believe it's warranted.

Vague Statements

Some people say cold reading involves making vague statements that could be interpreted to mean almost anything. Wrong.

When people mention 'vague statements', they are usually referring to what are known as 'Barnum statements'. These are statements that could apply to lots of people but, in the context of a reading, sound quite specific and meaningful to the client. One example is, 'Disciplined and self-controlled outside, you tend to be worrisome and insecure inside.' If you want to know more, you can go online and read about 'The Barnum Effect' or 'The Forer Effect'.

It's *possible* to give a reading to someone relying almost entirely on Barnum statements. However, the reading will be flat, limited and unlikely to impress anyone. The truth is that Barnum statements are only a small part of cold reading technique and not a particularly persuasive or interesting one.

Fishing For Clues

I've heard it said that cold reading relies on the readers 'fishing for clues'. Wrong again.

If you're any good at cold reading, you never need to 'fish for clues' because it's completely unnecessary and doesn't help. You can give a client a perfectly good, satisfactory reading without knowing anything about them and without needing to ask even a single question. It's true that there are subtle and sneaky ways to obtain information from clients if that's what you want to do. We discuss these a lot down at The Magic Circle! However, none of these methods could fairly be described as 'fishing for clues'. This is far too simplistic. It would be like saying the secret to heart bypass surgery is having a sharp knife.

Reading Body Language

Another popular trope is that successful cold reading involves reading body language. Yet again, wrong.

First of all, it's possible to give perfectly good readings to clients you can't see (for example, some people give readings over the phone). However, even when the reader can see the client, giving a reading has precious little to do with body language. Quite simply, cold reading and how to read body language are two separate fields of study, like carpentry and country dancing. You can be superb at one and know next to nothing about the other.

I've given hundreds of readings without paying any attention whatsoever to the client's body language. In addition, I'm fortunate enough to have met or worked with some of the world's leading body language experts, such as Joe Navarro (author of 'What Every Body Is Saying'), Chase Hughes ('The Ellipsis Manual') and Peter Collett ('The Book Of Tells'). I heartily recommend the work of these three brilliant authors. You should read their books, attend their lectures and go on their courses. You'll learn a great deal worth learning.

However, I can safely say that none of the techniques and methods these experts teach would help anyone to give a successful personal reading. To repeat for emphasis: cold reading and how to read body language are two *separate* subjects. Knowing about one doesn't inform you about the other. .

Copying Sherlock Holmes

The commonest misconception about cold reading is that it involves observing small details about the client and making keen deductions in the style of Sherlock Holmes. This is more wrong than King Wrong of Wrong Land on 'Let's Be More Wrong Than Ever' day. There is simply no connection whatsoever between Sherlock-style deductions and cold reading.

I apologise for the fact that the following section is quite lengthy. However, this misunderstanding about Sherlock Holmes comes up so often that I'd like to at least try to lay it to rest once and for all. In fact, I'd like to bury it in concrete and tip it down an active volcano.

Fiction Isn't Fact

In the brilliant Sherlock Holmes stories by Sir Arthur Conan Doyle, the author describes the great detective's ability to look at someone, notice small clues and make astonishing deductions. Conan Doyle's descriptions of the great detective's methods are highly entertaining. However, they have nothing to do with cold reading. What's more, they have nothing to do with real life. The brilliant deductions, though fun to read, do not withstand close scrutiny.

For example, in 'The Sign Of Four', Holmes deduces that his friend Dr. Watson has been inside the Wigmore Street Post Office. How did he know? He says that some dirt near the post office has a distinctive reddish hue and there's a trace of it on Watson's shoe. However, the dirt could in fact have ended up on Watson's shoe in several different ways. Maybe a dog got some of this reddish dirt on its paws then later got in Watson's way and brushed by his shoe. Who knows?

I *know* that these are great stories and can be enjoyed as such. I'm just pointing out that the deductions featured in the stories wouldn't work in real life. In Terry Pratchett's novel 'Feet Of Clay', a character called Samuel Vimes ridicules this type of crime story deduction. He says these passages are written as if *every* effect has only one possible cause when in fact human existence is much more varied than this. Any author writing a story can make sure the detective's deductions are impressively correct. Unfortunately, we don't live in a fictional realm full of pleasantly contrived victories. The real world is never quite so kind and accommodating.

It Doesn't Work In Real Life

Can anyone in real life make amazing deductions in the style of Sherlock Holmes? I'm not aware of any good reason to believe that this is the case. I know a large number of people with strange, curious and intriguing skills. However, I've never seen any credible evidence of this specific talent.

People who disagree with me on this sometimes refer me to videos they've seen of mindreaders in action. For example, they might have seen a video where a mindreader seems able to guess what someone does for a living just by observing them closely. I've no wish to spoil the party, but the mindreader isn't *really* relying on subtle visual clues to reach their conclusions. What you're watching is a magic trick, like sawing a lady in half.

This type of magical entertainment is called 'mentalism', meaning the type of magic that looks like mindreading or psychic ability. If you'll forgive my saying so, I'm an expert in this field (credentials on request). If you see anyone giving the type of demonstration I've referred to, there's a strong chance that they are friends of mine. I promise that what you're seeing is mentalism, not deduction.

Obvious V. Reliable

Here's one final point about the 'subtle clues' theory. It's true that someone giving a reading might look at the client now and again to glean useful information. However, this is at best only a minor part of good cold reading technique. The reason is that reliable observations tend to be obvious while observations that aren't obvious tend not to be all that reliable.

Suppose I'm giving a reading to someone who is clearly in the peak of physical fitness. She's wearing casual sports wear including a T-shirt from a popular local gym. It's fair to deduce that she has a keen interest in health and fitness. During my reading, I could make a few statements to this effect. However, the client would know perfectly well how I reached this conclusion.

The myth that cold reading involves shrewd deductions in the style of Sherlock Holmes is remarkably and unhelpfully persistent. I hope I've been able to finally lay it to rest.

How It Works

We've looked at a few ways in which cold reading *doesn't* work (vague statements, fishing for clues, body language, pretending to be Sherlock Holmes). Now let's take a brief look at how it *does* work. I apologise for the repetition, but I have to emphasise that this is only a brief and necessarily superficial introduction to how cold reading works. It's a huge subject and in a single chapter like this I can only cover the basics.

First of all, I'm going to talk about how cold reading works in the context of the psychic industry. Then I'll talk about how you can apply cold reading techniques to business contexts that have nothing to do with 'fortune-telling'. Just before we get to the mechanics, let's take a brief detour to discuss ethics.

Ethics

Some readers believe they have a real psychic gift and that the belief system they work with, such as tarot cards, provides genuine psychic or mystical insight. Within the trade, these are known as 'shut eyes', meaning they sincerely believe in what they do (although a sceptic

Teaching a small cold reading class in London

would suggest, in their typically boring way, that they are mistaken). Other readers are known as 'open eyes', meaning they don't believe they have a psychic talent but they are happy to play the part. They might do this because they enjoy giving readings or because it pays the bills. You can condemn this as deceptive or exploitative but this isn't necessarily the case. Sometimes, giving someone a reading is a way to give them a sense of hope or to help them feel more confident. It has been described as 'the poor man's psychotherapy'.

There is no doubt that cold reading *can* be used for unethical and nefarious purposes. For example, in the course of a tarot reading, the reader might tell the client that she's been having bad luck recently because someone has put an evil curse on her. The reader says she can 'lift' the curse but it will cost £1000 and she ought to pay up quickly 'before things get a lot worse'. I've heard *stories* of this type of thing going on but can't say for sure that it happens in real life. Nonetheless, such stories are often paraded as evidence of the type of abuse that lurks within some corners of the psychic industry.

It would be wrong to conclude that cold reading is inherently wrong in ethical terms. Like a sharp knife, it can be used with good intentions or harmful ones. There are people who give free readings simply as a form of entertainment that helps people to feel good about themselves. One can argue that *anything* that promotes belief in pseudo-scientific attitudes or mysticism pollutes the cultural stream from which we all drink. These ethical debates have been going round in circles for a long time and will doubtless continue to do so.

Let's move on from ethics to mechanics.

Many Options, Many Styles

It is definitely *not* the case that everyone who practises cold reading uses the same techniques in the same way. You could almost say there are as many different approaches to cold reading as there are people who give readings.

The simplest approach is the 'this means x' school of readings. The would-be tarot reader buys a deck of tarot cards and studies the booklet that comes with it. (I'm using the female pronoun because the vast majority of people who give readings are women.) This booklet ascribes a particular meaning to each of the 78 cards in the deck, such as, 'The four of wands implies learning and the pursuit of new knowledge'. (This is a made-up example). Having learned what each of the 78 cards supposedly means, the reader can then offer readings. A client comes along and chooses a few cards from the tarot deck. The reader turns over each card, says 'this card means x' and does her best to provide an engaging and interesting reading.

Another approach involves a 'key' or 'trigger' system. Here's a very simple example. The reader learns 26 good cold reading lines and associates each one with a letter of the alphabet. Thus prepared, she goes to a party or social event where she has been asked to give short readings to people as a form of 'walkabout' entertainment. Each time she gives a reading to someone, she starts by asking their name and ascertaining their initials. She can then provide a short reading based largely on whichever two lines she associates with those letters in her system. At a formal corporate event, people might be wearing badges or lanyards with their name on, thus making the process a little easier. This is a simple example and key systems can be much more elaborate than this. However, the basic idea is the same: base the reading around given details that produce a different permutation of lines in every case. Of course, there's a limit to the number of permutations (676 in this case) but this is rarely if ever likely to be a problem.

A third approach to cold reading involves learning a large number of what are called stock lines, or 'stocks' for short. Some readers make it their business to learn sets of stocks, each being suitable for a different demographic such as 'young female', 'middle-aged male', 'young couple' and so on (sometimes couples go for readings together). Over a period of time, the reader builds up a working repertoire of stock lines for each of these demographics. She can get stock lines from books or other practitioners but for the most part she acquires them via practical experience. If a reader tries a line a few times and finds it is generally well received, she adds this to her repertoire of 'greatest hits', her mental 'box of stocks'. Some readers I know have memorised dozens of stock lines to suit every possible group and occasion.

Totally Improvised Readings

My own approach to cold reading is the one that I teach in my book, 'Super Psychic Readings'. (I have already explained this but I need to pause to do so again. I included 'psychic' in the title so people would know what it's about. In real life, I never use the word 'psychic' and I call them 'personal' readings instead.)

My system has nothing to do with 'this means x', keys or stock lines. It is an entirely *improvised* system. You can use this system to give a reading based on any belief system you wish: tarot, palmistry, graphology (handwriting), astrology, spiritualism or anything else. The *presentational* aspects of the readings change but the underlying system remains the same.

When I teach my system, I break down the preparation for giving a reading into four areas: props, acting, ritual and terminology. Then I explain how to actually find things to say. This comes down to themes, statements and revisions.

1. Themes

There are a number of subjects (or themes, as I call them) that experience suggests people like to hear about. Four of the most common ones are Career, Health, Relationships and Money (easily remembered as 'CHaRM'). Three other good themes are Travel, Education and Aspirations ('TEA'). There are many other themes readers can use but even these seven are enough to fuel a thousand perfectly good readings.

In the course of giving a reading, the reader can use as few or as many of these themes as they want, in any order. I've given readings that were more or less all about one theme. I've given others that involved four or five.

These themes all overlap. For example, your career can affect your health, travelling is a form of education and money can be a source of dispute in relationships. Each theme is also open to broad interpretation. 'Career' doesn't just mean 'what the client does for a living'. The reader could talk about careers the client has considered but rejected, or would one day like to pursue, or why choosing a career was a challenge. Each theme offers numerous different avenues to explore.

2. Statements

So far, so good. The reader knows several themes that tend to provide a good basis for a reading.

Next, the reader has to know how to make a statement that will sound non-obvious yet plausible, and that the client will probably accept as right or mostly right. I have two approaches to this. In the 'Super Psychic Readings' book, which aims to be simple and pragmatic rather than comprehensive, I provide just four basic templates for plausible statements. In my larger book, 'The Full Facts Book of Cold Reading', I list 38 different 'elements' or types of statements you can use when giving a reading. These are divided into four categories:

- Character and personality.

- Facts and events in the client's life.

- Extracting information (in subtle ways).

- The future.

Let me share a couple of examples. The 'character and personality' group of elements includes what I call the 'Rainbow Ruse'. This credits the client with both a personality trait and its opposite, like this:

'You can be a considerate person at times — thoughtful and quick to provide for others. However, if you're completely honest, there are times when you do recognise a slightly selfish streak in yourself.'

In the context of a reading most clients will accept this as a perceptive insight into their personality and their life. (If they do not accept it, this isn't a problem. See the next section on 'Revisions'.) Here's another example of the type of statement readers can use. In my 'facts and events' group is one called 'A Childhood Memory'. This involves referring to a creative or artistic talent that the client didn't pursue in adult life:

'In your younger years, I sense a particular interest or subject you were keen on, maybe on the creative or artistic side. You showed promise and your parents or teachers felt you might go on to great things, but it was not to be.'

Most clients accept this statement and will readily offer additional details, such as saying they loved painting or playing the piano. If the client rejects this statement, I know they almost certainly loved a physical activity instead, such as sport or dancing.

Please excuse me labouring this point but it's important: these are just two examples of the types of statements that one can use during a personal reading. There are at least 36 others.

When the reader offers a statement that the client accepts, the reading can of course proceed happily and successfully. However, what happens if the client disagrees and *rejects* a statement? Fortunately, this doesn't matter and in fact makes no difference to the success of the reading. The next section explains why.

Demonstrating and teaching cold reading at a large conference in Orlando, Florida

3. Revisions

When the reader offers a statement, the client will either accept it or reject it. If the client feels the statement is right (or mostly right), the reader has succeeded in their goal. They have managed to make a correct statement to a complete stranger. The client is going to go away feeling impressed and satisfied.

What if the client rejects the statement? First of all, they are unlikely to do this very strenuously. People who go for readings *want* the reading to go well because they've invested their time, money and belief in it. This being the case, they tend to give the reader the benefit of the doubt. They generally let an inaccurate statement pass by and wait for whatever the reader says next. Even if they do reject a statement, they tend to do so quite gently: "Well, I wouldn't say that's *quite* right but, mm... I can maybe see what you mean."

However, even if a client does flatly reject a statement, this isn't a problem. It's always possible to *revise* a statement so it doesn't seem incorrect at all. Consider this example from a tarot reading:

> "The cards suggest that you've recently been promoted at work or taken on some new responsibilities."
>
> "No. That's wrong. Same job, no change whatsoever."
>
> "Okay, that's fine. However, there are indications here of the type of change I mentioned — a promotion or a new role for you. So if that hasn't happened yet, I expect it's coming up quite soon, or at least there will be an *opportunity* to take on a new role. So, look out for that, will you? And be ready to take full advantage of the opportunity when it turns up."

This is an example of what I call a Time Revision. It involves revising the original statement, which referred to the *present*, so that it now refers to the *future* and to potential events. In this way, the incorrect statement becomes magically transformed into a correct one — or, at least, one that can't yet be declared as either correct or incorrect.

Part of the power of cold reading derives from the fact that the client never knows what the reader would have said if they'd given a different response. Imagine a 'psychic' is giving a reading and simply takes a wild guess: "I'm getting a sense that I should talk to you about someone called Kate or Katherine or a name like that. This name means something to you, doesn't it?" If the client happens to know someone with this name, or a similar name, they will be astonished. "That's my sister's name!" they'll reply. Afterwards, the client will tell their friends, "It was amazing! I went to see this psychic and she instantly got my sister's name! How did he know?". Another victory for the intriguing powers of the psychic realm.

This guess will sound impressive regardless of the closeness of the relationship. To somehow 'sense' the name of the client's sister or an immediate relative seems impressive. However, if Katherine happens to be the client's spouse's second cousin, this might feel even *more* impressive. It implies that the tendrils of psychic insight can extend to the furthest reaches of the client's family tree.

If the client can't place anyone called Katherine, the reader can say, "Ah, well if that name doesn't mean anything to you at the moment, it will do soon. Will you watch out for that? This is going to be an important connection for you." This is the Time Revision again.

Alternatively, the reader can say, "Well, if that name doesn't mean anything to *you*, it's definitely a significant name for someone close to you or close to your heart. Anyway, the point is, this person's influence is going to be benign and is to be encouraged."

This is what I call the Apply Revision. The basic pattern is, 'If the statement doesn't apply to you [the client] then it must apply to someone near or close to you'. The client simply never knows what the reader or 'psychic' would have said if they had replied differently.

When I teach cold reading, I teach seven revisions in all. This is why, if you're adept at cold reading, you can make statements to complete strangers for the rest of your life without ever being wrong. During the many years that I worked in sales, I found this rather useful.

The Desire To Believe

So far, in this skim across the surface of how cold reading works, we've looked at themes, statements and revisions and how they fit together. This brings us to the final, essential element of the cold reading process: the desire to believe.

Throughout history, people have been keen to gain knowledge and power that the frustratingly limited natural world can't provide. This desire has given rise to numerous types of superstitious thinking and supernatural beliefs. For a comprehensive account of this process, I highly recommend Daniel O'Keefe's superb book, 'Stolen Lightning: The Social Theory of Magic'. It is simply brilliant.

This predisposition to believe means that so long as the reader looks and acts the part, and allows the client to *feel* they are taking part in a meaningful process, the client will probably be satisfied with their reading. They are likely to perceive meaning and significance in the reading in the same way that people see castles in clouds or faces in almost everything. (This is called pareidolia. There are wonderful sets of examples online.)

As well as the predisposition to believe, the cold reading process is also greatly assisted by confirmation bias. This is the tendency to accept anything that fits what you want to believe and reject everything else. (We looked at this in Chapter 13, which was all about disagreement.) Let's say that, while giving a reading, the reader offers four correct statements, four incorrect ones and a couple that are half-right if the client interprets them creatively. Afterwards, the client is likely to only remember and talk about the statements that were right or half-right. The errors, mistakes and misses simply get forgotten or dismissed as unimportant.

This concludes my brief survey of cold reading techniques. We've looked at simple 'x means y', stock and key systems. We've also looked (briefly) at the wholly improvised approach, which I happen to prefer because it's more versatile.

Cold Reading For Business

I spent many years of my life in the delightful world of sales and marketing, chiefly on the creative side. I loved this work. There's a certain joy in helping companies to shape and refine their message so that their marketing actually works and delivers results. After a few years in this line of work, and having done a fair bit of business-to-business (B2B) selling myself, I realised that I could combine two of my passions. I saw that it's possible to apply some of the underlying communication psychology of cold reading to areas such as sales and management.

At first, you may feel rather sceptical about this suggestion. I agree that, on the surface, there doesn't seem to be much of a connection between a tarot reading and, say, a typical B2B sales visit. However, let's explore this notion in a little more detail.

Imagine that a client goes along for a tarot card reading. The reader goes through the usual process and gets to the point where a few cards have been chosen and laid out. The reader peers at the cards for a second and then says something like, "There's an indication here that health issues have been on your mind... perhaps a back problem or something of that nature?" We'll assume that the client accepts this as correct or mostly correct.

Let's freeze the action at this point to ask an interesting question. What has the person giving the reading achieved in the space of about thirty seconds? She has:

- Established **credibility** for herself and whatever divinatory system is on offer (in this case tarot).

- Established her **role** and profile (how she wants the client to think of her).

- Made the client feel **important** and the centre of attention.

- Shown **empathy** with the client's problems.

- Created a sense of **trust** and cooperation, hence created good **rapport**.

- Created a **positive** tone of insight and reassurance.

It's really rather remarkable that the reader can achieve all of these things so rapidly. I'm not aware of any alternative approach or way of thinking about communication that can achieve so much, so quickly. The essence of the appeal of this process is the empathic offering of a statement, pertaining to a problem, that the client accepts as accurate and helpful. In this scenario, the insight is supposed to come from the power of the tarot as an oracle, a source of insight, and the reader's ability to interpret the cards successfully.

Let's start to apply or transplant some of this same communication psychology to a typical B2B sales visit.

In the scene I've just described, the reader rapidly established her *credibility* (as a provider of psychic insight) and the credibility of the system. She mainly achieved this by quickly getting to what sounded like proof of her insight: the *statement* about the client's health and the specific reference to back pain. The client could *relate* to this and accept it as correct or mostly correct.

Giving astrological readings to two clients for BBC TV

In a B2B sales scenario, you can rapidly establish your credibility, and the credibility of your company, in a similar way. One way to do this is to say something that shows the OP you know about their company, industry or market, including recent developments, and understand some of the problems they currently face.

There are two ways to make a statement of this kind. The first way is to go into the meeting fully briefed and immaculately prepared, having done all of your background research. This is clearly the ideal scenario. However, in the real world, this isn't always possible. Sometimes, you have to go into your sales visit or meeting less than perfectly prepared. In this situation, it's reassuring to know that you can *still* say something that sounds full of insight and that the client will be able to relate to. Cold reading enables you to do this.

The point is not to *con* the prospect or *fool* them into thinking you know more than you do. The point is not to try to bluff your way through the meeting. The point is to arm yourself with as many good ways as possible to foster rapport and build strong business relationships — even if the circumstances are less than ideal. Your aim is to provide what the client wants, which is sense that you can *relate* to them and you're on the same wavelength. People like to feel understood and that they don't have the face their problems alone.

Here's another aspect of the tarot comparison. In the tarot scenario, the reader defined and established her *role* very clearly ('person who can interpret the cards and provide psychic insight'). She did this by looking, acting and sounding the part and by being able to offer what sounded like a meaningful statement with a tone of sensitivity and concern. During a B2B sales visit, you can do the same to define your role, in the OP's perception, as someone who is well informed, aware of their problems and able to solve them.

The tarot reader showed *empathy* with the client's problems by mentioning her lower back pain (at least, that's how the client will remember it). In a sales situation, you can achieve the same feeling of empathy by mentioning a problem or challenge that the OP is concerned about. With cold reading, you can do this even if, as it happens, you don't have a great deal of information to go on.

While this is only a brief summary, I hope you can begin to see that there are some useful parallels between the two scenarios.

When I teach CRFB, I break it down into a four steps (DESA):

- Define you role and how you want to be perceived.

- Empathise: identify a problem the OP has to contend with (even if you know very little about their business).

- Statement: make a statement about this problem that the OP can relate to and will accept as insightful and relevant.

- Advance: use this to advance the conversation in the direction you want, such as, '…and that's why I wanted to show you what our new software can do for you'.

This is only a very bare overview of the process. The part of the class where we focus on developing empathy is usually one of the most interesting and rewarding. I start by taking the students through a few real-life case studies where we look at different businesses and try to empathise with the business owner's main problems or concerns. I then encourage attendees to come up with their own examples, which can be hypothetical or based on real-life situations they've come across. I don't think anyone can be *less* successful in business by learning *more* about empathy.

The objection about 'trying to con the OP' comes up sufficiently often as to be worth addressing again. CRFB is not about trying to fool anyone into thinking you know more than you do, although I accept this might be an incidental by-product of the process.

The first point of CRFB is to give yourself the reassurance of knowing that *even if* you have to make the sales visit while less than perfectly prepared — possibly through no fault of your own — you can still make an excellent impression. The second point is to equip yourself with a structured, strategic way to foster rapport by making insightful statements the OP can *relate* to. The third point is to teach empathic thinking, to get sales people to step into the mind of the OP and see their business problems from their point of view.

To be clear, I am suggesting that cold reading is a useful *addition* to your normal sales technique, not a *replacement* for it. The ability to make emotionally meaningful statements to a prospect is immensely useful in terms of building a good relationship with them.

Of course, cold reading will always principally be associated with the worldwide 'psychic' industry and the business of giving personal readings. This remarkable industry has been thriving for centuries, in one form or another, and I've no doubt will continue to do so. However, I love applying the basic skills of cold reading to other contexts that have nothing to do with giving readings. It's a truly wonderful communication skill and it would be a shame for people not to recognise its broader potential.

Chapter Summary

This chapter was all about the fascinating world of cold reading. The main headings were:

- A working definition.

- Four misconceptions. (Vagueness / Fishing / Body language / Sherlock.)

- How it works. (Themes / Statements / Revisions / The desire to believe.)

- Cold reading for business.

This concludes the third main chapter of Part Four.

DUCK

Four Books (One Of Which Is Free)

I've written three books on cold reading. They all serve a slightly different purpose. Available from my website or Amazon.

1. 'The Full Facts Book Of Cold Reading'. This describes how cold reading works in the psychic industry. It's a descriptive book, not a prescriptive one. It doesn't teach you how to give readings. Some people, including top UK mentalist Derren Brown, have been kind enough to call this the 'definitive' book on cold reading.

2. 'Super Psychic Readings'. This teaches you my system for giving any type of reading you want, to anyone, anywhere. It also includes stories about readings I've given all around the world in various interesting situations.

3. 'Cold Reading For Business'. This describes how to take some principles of cold reading and apply them to business contexts, especially selling, management and any situation where you would like to be more persuasive.

I've also written a booklet called 'A Simple Introduction To Cold Reading'. You can get this as a free instant download from my website (ianrowland.com/peoplejoy). There is some overlap between that booklet and the material in this chapter.

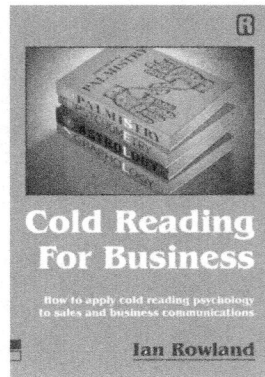

The Full Facts Book Of
Cold Reading

The definitive guide to cold reading
techniques used in the psychic industry

Ian Rowland

**Super Psychic
Readings**

A complete system for giving
any type of personal reading

Ian Rowland

**Cold Reading
For Business**

How to apply cold reading psychology
to sales and business communications

Ian Rowland

Developing Your Interest

There are many other sources of information on cold reading. First and foremost, I recommend any of the many books written by my prolific and wonderful friend Richard Webster. All of his work is excellent and worth studying.

'The Tarot Reader's Notebook' by Ron Martin is one of the best books on cold reading ever written. I also recommend 'The Dance' by my friend Brad Henderson, which largely focuses on the psychological interplay between the reader and the client.

If you go to the Penguin Magic website, you can download a lecture by my friend Krystyn Lambert about her compassion-based approach to cold reading and how she uses it as an element in her stage show. Krystyn is a delightful person, as well as being a very gifted magician and entertainer. I'm proud to count her among my friends in the magic community.

If you're interested in cold reading, I have two suggestions for you.

First of all, *please* get your information from people who actually give convincing readings to strangers in real life. I'm not trying to disparage books, lectures and courses by people who either can't or don't give readings. I'm sure they have some value to offer. However, I think that in some cases they spread more fog than light. My advice is always to learn from people who can and do give readings. I won't say 'if they can't do it, they can't teach it'. I will say they can't teach it *as well* as people with plenty of practical experience.

Secondly, please appreciate that you can only gain proficiency in cold reading by doing it. More to the point, by doing it *frequently*. Books can explain the basic principles. Classes and courses can provide a safe environment in which to learn and practise (and can be great fun). However, there is only one way to develop any degree of expertise: give readings to people, and plenty of them, over a period of several years. You have to build up your experience or, as we say in the magic community, your 'flying time'.

18. Love Is What Works

"One's life has value so long as one attributes value to the life of others, by means of love, friendship, and compassion"

— Simone de Beauvoir

Love Is What Works

As you know, there are many definitions of love. My preferred version is brief and pragmatic:

Love is what works.

It works better than anything else we've ever tried.

The 1487 publication, 'Malleus maleficarum', stated that seizures and fits were proof that someone was a witch. This led to many innocent women being hanged or burned alive. Today, we understand what causes epilepsy and that there are no witches in the supernatural sense. We managed to escape the snarling murk of ignorance because a few people loved knowledge enough to make the effort to obtain it. We also learned to love and accept people instead of demonising them and blaming them for things that weren't their fault.

In the 1960s, if a child had dyslexia the teacher would smack their hands with a ruler and tell them off for not trying hard enough to read. This attitude involved blame and violence and didn't work. It never helped a single child to read but did make them feel inferior. How were we able to progress past this stage? Again, because some people loved knowledge enough to do the research to obtain it. Today, we understand dyslexia and know that differences in brains and brain chemistry mean we're all innately good (or bad) at different things. We also stopped hurting and blaming and learned to add some love and understanding to the way we teach children to read.

Love is what works. I'm referring to the love of knowledge, love of people and love of progress instead of ignorance, blame and hurt. The lack of love diverts us from our potential and corrodes our belief in our self-greatness, individually and collectively. Of course, an attitude or policy of love can easily be dismissed as spiritual verbiage, an overly poetic outlook or a retreat into 'hippy' pacifism. Personally, I see it as a taste for pragmatism.

Some people have a vested interest in caustic tribalism. They toil in the trade of 'us against them', parading stale and squalid tropes of 'divide and conquer'. The leader of Tribe 1 says: "We are the good people. All the problems are caused by those bad people in Tribe 2. We must blame them and keep the nice things for ourselves. Vote for me." Meanwhile, the leader of Tribe 2 says the exact opposite.

I think it would be all right if we all said we're bored with this now. It's been going on a long time and adds to problems rather than solving them. The time has come for the clever apes to finally progress past tribalism. This is our next great step forward, after agriculture, steam power and the microchip. It's time to reflect on witch hunts and dyslexia and wonder where else we might be blaming the victim. Do some innately bad people cause problems in society? Or does society cause bad problems for some people?

We're all just people. We are a walking collage of random factors such as genes, geography and genius (or the lack of it). We eat, sleep and breathe. Each day, we do the best we can with what we've got, being innately good at some things more than others for reasons we didn't choose. We try to move towards what feels good and away from what feels bad, which isn't easy because life can be prickly, unkind and unfair. This is your story, my story, everyone's story.

We don't have to sort ourselves into people bundles marked 'us' and 'them'. It would be better to embrace the glorious truth of our sameness and lend one another a hand. It's good to love and be loved. It's good to be the helper and the helped.

Love works better than tribalism, anger, blame, ignorance, hate and hurt. To see the truth, you don't have to invoke textual tapestries of religious, spiritual or mystical insight (although I know some find these presentations appealing). You just have to look around you. I believe that loving one another involves learning how to talk to one another successfully and then making the effort to do so. This takes us all in a good direction — one where we can all find and share People Joy.

Find the joy in people. Find it in yourself. Find it in what works.

Thank you for reading People Joy. I hope that you and I can meet one day. I'd love to talk with you!

In Conclusion

If a book can be described as a 'conversation' between writer and reader, then this brings us to the end of our *current* conversation. I hope it won't be our last.

I hope you gained some value from this book and that you'll tell other people about it. My only sales team is you.

If you'd like to get in touch, I'd love to hear from you. My contact details are below and you can also find me on Facebook.

Thank you for reading People Joy.

— Ian Rowland

London, 2025

Email address: ian@ianrowland.com
Website: www.ianrowland.com
Or sub-section: www.ianrowland.com/peoplejoy

Let's Work Together!

What Problem Can I Solve For You?

You can hire me for your conference or company event. I offer keynotes, talks and training on various aspects of People Joy — with *or* without a touch of magical entertainment.

You can hire me to train your group, team or department.

You can hire me for some one-on-one training, online or in person.

Get in touch and let's see what problem I can solve for you. I'd love to talk with you!

Details, credentials, testimonials: www.ianrowland.com .

To date, I've been hired by the FBI, Google, Coca-Cola, Marks & Spencer, the British Olympics Team, the Ministry of Defence, Hewlett-Packard, The Philadelphia 76ers, CapGemini, BBC, Kier Construction, NBC, The Crown Estate, Iceland, Unilever, the Sunday Times Oxford Literary Festival, The Prince's Charities, McKinsey & Company, Eurostar Software Testing Conference, Ogilvy & Mather, London Business School... and many more.

I've also lectured at Oxford University, Cambridge University, the California Institute Of Technology and Monash University.

Thanks And Acknowledgements

"A friend may well be reckoned the
masterpiece of nature."

— R.W. Emerson

At a rough count, a thousand people contributed to this book in one way or another. I can't possibly thank or credit all of them. However, I'd like to send my love, thanks and gratitude to the following. All of these wonderful people, in various ways, either inspired People Joy or helped me to write it.

First of all, thank *you* for reading this book.

My parents, Joan and Des, passed away some years ago. They were the greatest parents in the world, of course, who gave me a good start in life and taught me many valuable lessons. They were the first to show me that love is what works.

My big brother Steve and my big sister Anne are both impressive and admirable people who have achieved a great deal. I look up to them with love, respect and admiration.

David Britland was my magical mentor and a valued source of advice and encouragement during my teenage years. I have no doubt that he contributed a great deal to my path through life. It was David who first got me into cold reading, so now you know who to blame.

JP Lodge expressed his belief in me at a time when this made a big difference to my future direction. His was the quiet voice that said "I believe in you". He was also lots of fun to know back when we both worked for the same company and he still is today!

I first had the pleasure of meeting Sam Qurashi many years ago when he hired me for some training. Before long, he became an immensely important friend and influence. Over the years, he has been not only a true friend but also a great source of support, fun, contacts and encouragement. In addition, there is no doubt among music scholars that our guitar jam sessions constitute the single greatest musical event in the history of ever.

Ian Kendall has been a dependably helpful friend for over 30 years. More specifically, in recent times he has become my unofficial, very patient and rock-solid source of tech support and desperately needed help with regard to all the software I use for projects such as this. Were it not for Ian's unfailingly patient help, I might never have managed to finish this book. He's also one of my favourite raconteurs, with an impressive gift for endless creative digression.

AJ Green has been a wonderful and very helpful friend for many years. He has helped me with numerous events and projects. Among other things, he has been my photographer, videographer and 'sound and lights' tech guy on more than a few occasions and has proved to be impressively dependable. As I've often said, there are three things you can rely on in life: tea, gravity and AJ Green.

I'm fortunate enough to have many funny, delightful and impressively talented friends in the worldwide magic community, including my friends in The Magic Circle in London. I'd like to thank them all for the good times we've shared. I hope there will be many more.

Matt Daniel-Baker, Chris Dodd and James Pritchard are three of my closest friends. They suffer from the terrible affliction of having exactly the same sense of humour as me. This is a heavy burden that they bear with fortitude. Thanks for all the good times, guys. I hope we'll be able to share many more.

I'd like to thank Oliver Tabor, Wayne Trice, Stu Turner and Alex Foden for their enduring friendship, help and support. I also feel immensely grateful to Liam Ball, John Duffett and the rest of the 'Friday night show' team for allowing me to be a small part of these truly magical evenings at TMC. It has been a genuine delight to work with you all and I look forward to doing so again.

Many of my friends contributed their time and knowledge to this project or supported it just by being good friends. My sincere thanks go to Linzi Allcock, Sonia Barton, Thom Bleasdale, Suzy Bryson and Adrian Plant, Michael Chaut, Andy Cooper, Jayne Corrigan, Bron Coveney (my favourite daytime TV expert), Joan DuKore, Susan Dynner, Max Fulham, Mikael Hedné, Katrina Kroetch, Krystyn Lambert, Akshay Laxman, Paul Longhurst, Lior Manor, Eva May Nicot, Liam O'Neill, Martin Pearce, Annette Rainbow, Katherine Rhodes, Romany, Jonathan Sabov, Stuart Scott, Suhani Shah, Reuel Singh and Scott Wells.

A few long-standing friends have somehow put up with me for tow, three or even four decades! They have all been a large part of 'People Joy'. I'd therefore like to offer special thanks to: James Batchelor, Reign Bowie, Uri Geller, Jaq Greenspon, Caroline Guirr and Tom Cantwell, Alan Jackson, Lynne Kelly, Isabel Losada, Rory Raven, Marika Rauscher, Angela Reader, Kate Saunders and Maria-Pia Taddei Boxley Streets. I'd also like to thank Cyndi Grady, Kathleen Hawkins and Kitty Mervine for their consistent friendship and support from 'across the pond'.

Thom Chesser is another of my valued friends in the magic world who also took care of the proofreading for this book. If you need a proofreader, he's the man to go to!

Lee Warren and Lee Hathaway inspire me by being incredibly good at what they do as well as being unfailingly great company. Our occasional dinners together are always hugely enjoyable and feature a feast of memorable stories.

A long time ago, JB of Child's Hill taught me a great deal about what it really feels like to love and be loved. I owe her a great deal.

When I started writing this book, I didn't know Alberto De Almeida. He turned up in one of my Facebook threads one day and we soon became friends. As I worked on this book, he helped with creative word-wrangling and painfully contrived acronyms. Alberto is partly responsible for the fact that there's a DUCK at the end of every chapter! If you see some creative wordplay in this book that you like, that's Alberto's work. If you dislike it, that's one of my bits.

John Kippen is someone else I got to know while I was writing this book. He's truly a remarkable man. I'd like to thank him for his kindness and for sharing his story and his inspiration.

Finally, I'd like to thank some of my heroes and inspirations, even though some have passed away and the rest will never know or care. These incredible people have shaped me, changed me and delighted me with their perfection: David Berglas, Truman Capote, Claudia Cardinale, Linda Eder, M.C. Escher, Donald Fagen, Martin Gardner, Dave Gilmour, Berry Gordy, Rita Hayworth, Mitch Hedberg, Joseph Heller, Jerome K. Jerome, Natasha Lyonne, Eric Morecambe, Bob Newhart, Mike Oldfield, Dorothy Parker, Cole Porter, Haley Reinhart, Chris Rock, Sting and Ana Vidovic.

Printed in Great Britain
by Amazon